faith first

Legacy Edition
PARISH

Grade Five

RCL✦
Benziger®

Cincinnati, Ohio

This book reflects the
new revision of the

ROMAN
MISSAL
THIRD EDITION

"The Ad Hoc Committee to Oversee the Use of the Catechism, United States Conference of Catholic Bishops, has found this catechetical series, copyright 2006, to be in conformity with the *Catechism of the Catholic Church*."

NIHIL OBSTAT
Reverend Robert M. Coerver
Censor Librorum

IMPRIMATUR
† Most Rev. Charles V. Grahmann
Bishop of Dallas

September 1, 2004

The Nihil Obstat and Imprimatur are official declarations that the material reviewed is free of doctrinal or moral error. No implication is contained therein that those granting the Nihil Obstat and Imprimatur agree with the contents, opinions, or statements expressed.

Send all inquiries to:
RCL Benziger
8805 Governor's Hill Drive
Suite 400
Cincinnati, Ohio 45249

Toll Free   877-275-4725
Fax   800-688-8356

Visit us at www.RCLBenziger.com
            www.FaithFirst.com

20475   ISBN 978-0-7829-1067-4 (Student Book)
20485   ISBN 978-0-7829-1079-7 (Catechist Guide)

ACKNOWLEDGMENTS

Scripture excerpts are taken or adapted from the *New American Bible with Revised New Testament and Psalms* Copyright © 1991, 1986, 1970, Confraternity of Christian Doctrine, Washington, DC. Used with permission. All rights reserved. No part of the *New American Bible* may be reproduced by any means without the permission of the copyright owner.

Excerpts are taken or adapted from the English translation of *Rite of Baptism for Children* © 1969, International Committee on English in the Liturgy, Inc. (ICEL); the English translation of the *Roman Missal* © 2010 ICEL; the English translation of the Act of Contrition from *Rite of Penance* © 1974, ICEL; the English translation of *Rite of Confirmation, Second Edition* © 1975, ICEL; the English translation of *The Ordination of Deacons, Priests, and Bishops* © 1975, ICEL; the English translation of *A Book of Prayers* © 1982, ICEL; the English translation of *Book of Blessings* © 1988, ICEL; *Catholic Household Blessings and Prayers* (revised edition) © 2007, United States Conference of Catholic Bishops, Washington, D.C. All rights reserved.

Excerpts are taken or adapted from the English translation of *Kyrie Eleison*, the *Nicene Creed*, the *Apostles' Creed*, *Sanctus and Benedictus*, *Agnus Dei*, *Gloria Patri*, and *Te Deum Laudamus* by the International Consultation on English Texts (ICET).

"Making All Things New," a Christmas tree blessing, page 248, adapted from the English translation of "Blessing of a Christmas Tree," *Book of Blessings* copyright © 1988, ICEL. All rights reserved.

Photography and Illustration Credits appear on page 304.

Faith First Legacy Edition
Development Team

Developing a religion program requires the gifts and talents of many individuals working together as a team. RCL Benziger is proud to acknowledge the contributions of these dedicated people.

Program Theology Consultants
Reverend Louis J. Cameli, S.T.D.
Reverend Robert D. Duggan, S.T.D.

Advisory Board
Judith Deckers, M.Ed.
Elaine McCarron, SCN, M.Div.
Marina Herrera, Ph.D.
Reverend Frank McNulty, S.T.D.
Reverend Ronald J. Nuzzi, Ph.D.

National Catechetical Advisor
Jacquie Jambor

Catechetical Specialist
Jo Rotunno

Contributing Writers
Student Book and Catechist Guide
Reverend Louis J. Cameli
Christina DeCamp
Judith Deckers
Mary Beth Jambor
Michele Norfleet

Art & Design Director
Lisa Brent

Electronic Page Makeup
Laura Fremder

Production Director
Jenna Nelson

Designers/Photo Research
Pat Bracken
Kristy O. Howard
Susan Smith

Project Editors
Patricia A. Classick
Steven M. Ellair
Ronald C. Lamping

Web Site Producers
Joseph Crisalli
Demere Henson

General Editor
Ed DeStefano

President/Publisher
Maryann Nead

Contents

We Celebrate: The Liturgical Seasons

We Pray

Dear God,
We can't believe we are finally in fifth grade! We are thankful for all the gifts you have given us. Help us to learn more about you this year and to be good followers of your Son, Jesus. We promise to love you and to treat your world and your people with care and respect. Amen.

Welcome to Faith First!

A Snapshot of Me

My name is _____.

The sacraments I have celebrated are _____

_____.

As a Christian, one thing I believe is _____

_____.

My Favorites

Animal _____

Bible story _____

Book _____

Snack _____

Music _____

Hobby _____

Movie _____

Celebrating Our Faith

Every year the Church helps us learn more about Jesus and his teachings. This year in fifth grade we will explore many ways that the Church celebrates the good news of our faith—the Resurrection of Jesus, the Light of the world.

Solve the Puzzle

This puzzle is a little bit like a crossword puzzle. Begin by solving the four clues in the boxes on page 9. Then transfer the letters of answers into the puzzle squares below with the corresponding numbers. The solution is a sentence that tells the main theme of the Gospel.

	9	14			20	8	5		16	1	19	3	8	1	12	
13	25	19	20	5	18	25		10	5	19	21	19				
16	1	19	19	5	4		6	18	15	13		12	9	6	5	
	20	8	18	15	21	7	8		4	5	1	20	8			
9	14	20	15		1		14	5	23		1	14	4			
7	12	15	18	9	15	21	19		12	9	6	5				

1. We Believe

This year in Unit 1 you will learn about the section of the Gospel that tells about a very important event in Jesus' life. The section is called the

___ ___ ___ ___ ___ ___ ___ narrative (see page 63).
16   1   19   19   9   15   14

2. We Worship

In Unit 2 you will learn much more about the Church's liturgy, the "work of the people" that we do when we worship God. The yearly cycle of the Church's celebration of the liturgy is called the

___ ___ ___ ___ ___ ___ ___ ___ ___ ___ year (see page 99).
12   9   20   21   18   7   9   3   1   12

3. We Live

The seven sacraments celebrate God's love for us. The Bible tells us how to respond to God's love. In the First Letter of

___ ___ ___ ___ we read,
10   15   8   14

"___ ___ ___ ___ ___ ___ ___ ___ ___ ___ ___ ___
23   8   15   5   22   5   18   12   15   22   5   19

___ ___ ___ ___ ___ ___ ___ ___ ___ ___ ___ love
7   15   4   13   21   19   20   1   12   19   15

___ ___ ___ ___ ___ ___ ___ ___ ___ ___" (see page 183).
8   9   19   2   18   15   20   8   5   18

4. We Pray

Because of all the gifts God has given us, Christians have a reason to celebrate every day. A way that the Church prays together around the clock every day of the year is called

___ ___ ___ ___ ___ ___ ___ ___ ___ ___ ___ ___
20   8   5   12   9   20   21   18   7   25   15   6

___ ___ ___ ___ ___ ___ ___ ___ (see page 221).
20   8   5   8   15   21   18   19

Your Word Is Light

The leader walks at the head of a procession to the prayer space, holding the Bible high for all to see.

All make the sign of the cross together.

LEADER: Lord, we gather today to honor you and to thank you for the gift of your word.

ALL: Your word is a light for our path.

LEADER: A reading from the Gospel according to Saint Matthew.

ALL: Glory to you, O Lord.

LEADER: *Proclaim Matthew 5:3–12.* The Gospel of the Lord.

ALL: Praise to you, Lord Jesus Christ.

LEADER: Lord Jesus, whenever we gather to hear your word, you are here with us. You are light for our path, and food for our spirit. Guide us as we continue our journey of faith this year.

ALL: Amen!

All come forward and bow before the Bible.

What does the Church ask us to believe?

Getting Ready

What I Have Learned

What is something you already know about these faith terms?

Divine Revelation

_____

_____

The Old Testament

_____

_____

The Marks of the Church

_____

_____

Words to Know

Put an X next to the faith terms you know. Put a ? next to the faith terms you need to know more about.

Faith Vocabulary

_X_ faith

____ Holy Trinity

_X_ Gospel

_X_ miracle

_X_ Lord

____ Paschal Mystery

____ Evangelists

____ charisms

____ Sacred Tradition

_X_ kingdom of God

Questions I Have

What questions would you like to ask about the work of the Holy Spirit in the Church?

_____

_____

_____

_____

A Scripture Story

Jesus and the disciples at sea

Why did Jesus perform miracles?

Speak, Lord

We Pray

Hallelujah!
Praise the LORD from
 the heavens;
 give praise in the
 heights.
Praise the LORD from
 the earth. PSALM 148:1, 7

I believe in one God.
I believe in one
 Lord, Jesus Christ.
I believe in the
 Holy Spirit. Amen.

What are some of the ways you come to know people better?

Sometimes, the more you learn about people, the more there is to know. The Holy Spirit continuously invites us to know and believe in God the Father, the Son, and the Holy Spirit.

What new things have you learned about God?

Divine Revelation

Faith Vocabulary

divine Revelation. God's making known over time the mystery of God and the divine plan of creation and salvation.

faith. A supernatural gift and power from God inviting us to know and believe in him and our free response to that invitation.

We Are Looking for God

There is a desire inside every person that makes us realize there is Someone much greater than we are. That Someone is God. That desire is part of who we are as human beings. Each of us is looking for God, and he is looking for us.

Saint Augustine, a bishop in the early Church, summarized our desire and our search for God. Augustine wrote:

You, O God, have made us for yourself, and our hearts are restless until they rest in you.

FROM CONFESSIONS

God's love for us is so great that he comes to us and invites us to know him, hope in him, and love him. It is the very reason God created us.

God Reveals Himself

How does God help us get to know him? The answer is: God reveals himself.

We cannot see God. We cannot know what is in God's mind. We cannot, on our own, come to know who God is and his plan of goodness for us and for the world. So God, out of love, revealed himself. **Divine Revelation** is God making himself and his plan of creation and salvation known.

God has revealed that he has created us. He is always inviting us to share in his life and love. Making God part of our lives, learning about him, and coming to know him bring us happiness. God wants us to be completely happy with him not only forever in heaven but also now on earth. That is why God created us.

What does it tell us about God that he reveals himself to us?

God Speaks Through Creation

One way God speaks to us is through his creation. God is the Creator who tells us about himself through the world we live in. When we look at creation, we realize how wonderful God is.

The sky, the stars, and the galaxies sing of God's love. The beauty of animals galloping on dry land, dolphins gliding through the waters, eagles soaring in the skies all reflect God's goodness and beauty. All creation gives honor and glory to God.

God Speaks Through People

One of the best ways God helps us know him is through people. Throughout the ages God has chosen special people through whom he revealed himself. In the Bible God tells us that the Israelites were the first people he chose. They would be his people, and he would be their God. The writer of the Book of Deuteronomy, the fifth book of the Bible, reminded the Israelites:

"[The Lord] has chosen you from all the nations on the face of the earth to be a people peculiarly his own." DEUTERONOMY 7:6

God was no stranger to his people. He was always present with them.

Faith-Filled People

Anselm of Canterbury

Saint Anselm was the archbishop of Canterbury, England. He is honored as one of the great theologians of the Church. A theologian is a person who studies and explains the faith so we can better understand what God has revealed. Anselm described his work as "faith seeking understanding." His feast day is April 21.

Notice the seal on this page. Design your seal to give praise to God.

Praise the Lord!

ALL THE EARTH, GIVE PRAISE TO GOD

15

Jesus, the Word of God

Title: Jesus

Write two words that describe the title.

_____ _____

Write three action words that describe the title.

_____ _____ _____

Write four words that tell a
feeling about the title.

_____ _____

_____ _____

Write another word for Jesus.

_____

God Reveals Himself Most Fully in Jesus

God revealed himself most fully in his only Son, Jesus Christ. Jesus is the Word of God. He is the Son of God who became one of us and lived among us.

Jesus spent his whole life on earth revealing God and God's love. Through all his actions and words we come to know God.

The Gift of Faith

God is always inviting us to come to know him and believe in him. He gives us the gift of **faith**. God also helps us listen to and say yes to that invitation. Faith is a supernatural gift and power that helps us respond to God's invitation with all our heart, our mind, our soul, and our strength.

The Holy Spirit helps us accept the gift of faith. As people of faith, we are the community of believers in Jesus Christ, the Church. When we accept and live the gift of faith, God works through us to help others come to know, love, and serve him.

A cinquain is a five-line verse. Follow the directions and write a cinquain about Jesus.

Pope John XXIII recording a radio and television address

Blessed John XXIII

The Catholic Church from its very beginning has had pastors who have guided the Church and others in the search for God. Blessed Pope John XXIII was one of those leaders.

Pope John XXIII called the Second Vatican Council that began in 1962. He called the Council to help the whole Church and the whole world better understand the meaning of God's revelation. He wanted the Church to be a clear and powerful sign of God's love in the world.

Pope John XXIII died on June 3, 1963. On September 3, 2000, Pope John Paul II named him Blessed John XXIII. This is the final step before naming a person a saint of the Church. Blessed John XXIII continues to inspire people to place their faith, hope, and love in God.

Who helps you better understand God's revelation and the Gospel? Who helps you live as a follower of Christ?

Pope John XXIII at prayer, Saint Peter's Basilica, Vatican City, Rome, Italy

CITTA' DEL VATICANO 1200

Reproduction of 1,200 lire (60 cent) stamp commemorating beatification of Pope John XXIII

What Difference Does Faith Make in My Life?

Every day the Holy Spirit is helping you come to know, love, and serve God better. Learning what the Church teaches will help you understand and live what God has revealed. It will help you grow as a child of God.

Place a check in the box next to the things you are doing to grow in your faith. Then write down other things you can do to come to know God better.

Learning More About God

☐ Reading the Bible

☒ Learning the teachings of the Church

☒ Praying to the Holy Spirit

☒ Thinking about God's gift of creation

Other things I can do are _____

_____.

Some people who can help me are _____

_____

_____

_____.

My Faith Choice

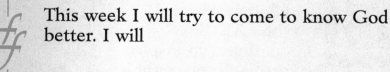

This week I will try to come to know God better. I will

_____

_____.

We Pray

Lord, Help Us Believe

Pray this act of faith. Ask God to help you come to know and believe in him better.

Leader: "Speak, LORD, for your servant is listening."

1 SAMUEL 3:9

All: "Speak, LORD, for your servant is listening."

Leader: Lord, help me come to know you better.

All: "Speak, LORD, for your servant is listening."

Leader: Lord, help me listen and say yes to your gift of faith.

All: "Speak, LORD, for your servant is listening."
Amen.

We Remember

Choose three of the faith terms in the word bank. Use each term in a sentence to describe how you come to know God.

**creation   people   Jesus Christ
faith   Church**

Some people have faith in Jesus Christ and pray at Church.

To Help You Remember

1. Divine Revelation is God making himself and his plan of creation and salvation known.

2. We can come to know God through creation and through people.

3. God most fully reveals himself in Jesus Christ, the Son of God who became one of us and lived among us.

This Week . . .

In chapter 1, "Speak, Lord," your child learned that there is a longing and a desire for God inside every person. God has revealed himself and gives us the gift of faith to know and respond to that desire. Creation points to the existence of a wise and loving and all-powerful God. Through the ages God has chosen special people through whom others can come to know, love, and serve him. Through them God has revealed his love for all people. In Jesus Christ, the Son of God who became one of us and lived among us, God has revealed himself most fully.

For more on the teachings of the Catholic Church on the mysteries of divine Revelation and the gift of faith, see *Catechism of the Catholic Church* paragraph numbers 50–67, 142–175, and 185–197.

Sharing God's Word

Invite all family members to share their favorite Bible story. Then talk about what each story tells about God. Emphasize that the Holy Spirit helps us know and believe in God.

Praying

In this chapter your child prayed an act of faith. Read and pray together this prayer on page 19.

Making a Difference

Choose one of the following activities to do as a family or design a similar activity of your own.

- Invite each person to share the names of people who have helped them know about God. Share how these people have helped. You might like to send notes thanking these people.

- Watch TV or look through magazines. Talk about what the commercials and advertisements tell us about happiness. How does this compare to the happiness God brings us?

- Blessed Pope John XXIII is remembered for his great love and compassion for all people. Choose one thing you can do to show your love and compassion for others.

For more ideas on ways your family can live your faith, visit the "Faith First for Families" page at **www.FaithFirst.com**. You will find the "About Your Child" page helpful as your child begins a new year.

The Word of God

We Pray

For the LORD's word
   is true;
   all his works are
      trustworthy. PSALM 33:4

Lord God,
send the Holy Spirit
to open my heart
   and mind
to your holy word.
                    Amen.

What is your favorite kind of book?

There are many types of books. The Bible is the most widely read book in the world. It is God's word.

What is your favorite story in the Bible?

Faith Focus

What kinds of writings are in the Bible?

Faith Vocabulary

inspiration of the Bible.
The Holy Spirit guiding the human writers of Sacred Scripture to faithfully and accurately communicate God's word.

Gospel. The Good News of God's love revealed in the life, death, Resurrection, and Ascension of Jesus Christ.

The Holy Writings of God

Books tell stories of happiness and sadness, successes and failures. The Bible tells the story of God's love for his people and their response to his love. The Bible is God's own word to us. God speaks through the Bible. Sacred Scripture is another name for the Bible. It is a name that means "holy writings." The Holy Spirit inspired, or helped, the human writers of the Bible to faithfully and accurately communicate God's word. We call this truth of our faith the **inspiration of the Bible.**

The Bible is a collection of many writings. The Church divides the Bible into the Old Testament and the New Testament. The word *testament* means "covenant." Guided by the Holy Spirit, the Church has identified the forty-six books of the Old Testament and the twenty-seven books of the New Testament to be the inspired word of God. We call this the canon of Scripture.

Do you know how to look up a Bible passage? Look up Mark 4:37–41. First decide whether the passage is in the Old Testament or the New Testament.

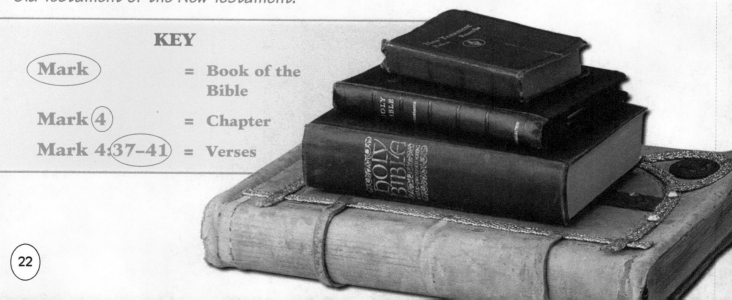

KEY

Mark = **Book of the Bible**

Mark ④ = **Chapter**

Mark 4:37–41 = **Verses**

The Old Testament

The Old Testament tells the story of the Covenant that God entered into with humankind. The story of the Covenant begins at creation. It continues with the stories of Noah and Abraham and Moses and the prophets. The Old Testament of the Bible has four different kinds of books, or writings.

The Torah

The Torah is the first five books of the Old Testament. These five books are also known as the Pentateuch, a word meaning "five containers." The Pentateuch contains the Commandments and laws that help God's people live the Covenant.

The Historical Books

There are sixteen historical books. They tell about the struggle of the Israelites to live the Covenant faithfully.

The Wisdom Writings

There are seven wisdom writings. They teach practical ways to live God's Law.

The Prophetic Books

There are eighteen prophetic books in the Old Testament. These books contain the teachings of the prophets. The prophets were people God chose to speak in his name.

The writers of the Bible told stories of God's people. You also have a faith story. Write a table of contents for your own faith story.

My Faith Story

The New Testament

Jesus is the new and everlasting Covenant. The New Testament reveals that Jesus Christ is the Son of God, the Savior and Redeemer of the world. Jesus most fully reveals, more than anyone else did or will ever do, God and his love for us. We divide the New Testament into four parts.

The Gospels

The four Gospels of Matthew, Mark, Luke, and John are the heart of the New Testament. Each **Gospel** shares, in its own way, the story and meaning of Jesus' life, Passion, death, Resurrection, and Ascension.

The Acts of the Apostles

The Acts of the Apostles is the story of how the Church began. It gives an account of the Apostles as they spread the good news of God's love and mercy revealed in Jesus Christ throughout the world.

The Letters

The twenty-one epistles, or letters, of Saint Paul the Apostle and other early Christian writers teach about Jesus and how Christians are to live.

The Book of Revelation

The Book of Revelation is the last book of the Bible. In it the Holy Spirit encourages Christians who are suffering to remain faithful to Jesus Christ.

Design this emblem with words and symbols for Jesus Christ.

Our Church Makes a Difference

Reverence for the Bible

The whole Christian life is strengthened by hearing and listening attentively and reverently to the word of God. Saint Jerome reminded us of the importance of the Bible in the life of Christians. He wrote, "Ignorance of the Scriptures is ignorance of Christ."

Before the printing press was invented in the sixteenth century, scribes copied the Bible by hand. Artists painted pages of the Bible with colors and decorated the edges of the pages with gold. Today the Bible is the most widely read book in the world.

Many Christian families have a family Bible. In it they write down the key events of their family's faith story. They record Baptisms, marriages, and other important milestones in the faith history of the family.

At every celebration of the Eucharist, we read the word of God aloud, or proclaim it. We carry the Book of the Gospels with dignity in the procession and proclaim the word of God from a place of honor. That place is called the ambo. This shows the faith of the Church in God's presence in his word.

When we gather with other members of the Church or as a family to read and listen to the Bible, Jesus is there. We listen and ask, What is God saying to us right now? How can the living word of God come alive in our lives today?

When does your family and parish listen to the word of God?

What Difference Does Faith Make in My Life?

As you listen to the word of God, the Holy Spirit helps you understand what God is saying to you. He gives you the knowledge and courage to put God's word into practice.

Look through your Bible. Take the time to become more familiar with the Old Testament and the New Testament. Select a passage, read it, and think about what God's word means for your life. Write your thoughts on these book pages.

God's Word Is Life-Giving

My Faith Choice

This week I will show that I believe it is important to listen to and live God's word. I will

_____

_____.

Your Word, Lord, Is a Light for My Path

Praying with the Bible is an important form of prayer of the Church. It is a form of meditation. We spend quiet time with God, reading and listening to his word and trying to understand how to live it.

1. Sit quietly. Close your eyes. Breathe slowly.

2. In your mind, picture yourself someplace where you can talk and listen to God.

3. Open your Bible and read a favorite passage.

4. Take time to talk and listen to God. Say, "Your word, Lord, is a light for my path" (based on Psalm 119:105).

5. After a few quiet moments, ask the Holy Spirit, "What is your word saying to me?" Write down any key words or phrases that you remember.

6. Make a faith decision to put God's word into action.

We Remember

Match the faith terms in the left column with the descriptions in the right column.

Terms

_____ 1. inspiration

_____ 2. Sacred Scripture

_____ 3. Pentateuch

_____ 4. Gospels

_____ 5. canon of Scripture

Descriptions

a. the first five books of the Old Testament

b. the list of inspired books named by the Church and collected in the Bible

c. the first four books of the New Testament

d. the holy writings of God

e. the help the Holy Spirit gave to the human writers of the Bible

To Help You Remember

1. The Bible is the inspired written word of God.

2. The Old Testament tells the story of God's Covenant with his people.

3. The New Testament reveals that Jesus Christ, the Son of God, is the new and everlasting Covenant.

This Week . . .

In chapter 2, "The Word of God," your child deepened his or her understanding of the Bible, or Sacred Scripture. The Bible contains the holy writings that the Holy Spirit inspired God's people to write. This list of writings named by the Church is called the canon of Scripture. The Old Testament tells the first part of the story of the Covenant that God made with people and his promise to send a messiah and savior. The New Testament tells about the fulfillment of God's promise and the new and everlasting Covenant that God made with all people in Jesus Christ.

For more on the teachings of the Catholic Church on Sacred Scripture, see *Catechism of the Catholic Church* paragraph numbers 50–133.

Sharing God's Word

Read together 1 Thessalonians 2:13 and 2 Timothy 3:16–17. Emphasize that the Bible is God's word to us.

Praying

In this chapter your child prayed a form of meditation called lectio divina. Read and pray together this prayer on page 27.

Making a Difference

Choose one of the following activities to do as a family or design a similar activity of your own.

- Talk with each other about how the Bible can help guide us. How is the Bible a light for our path?

- Choose a Bible story that you are familiar with. Find it in the Bible and read it together.

- Invite each person to share the name of a favorite person in the Bible. Share with each other the stories about these people.

For more ideas on ways your family can live your faith, visit the "Faith First for Families" page at **www.FaithFirst.com**. Click on "Bible Stories" and discuss the Bible story with your child this week.

The Mystery of the Holy Trinity

3

We Pray

"Come," says my heart,
   "seek God's face";
your face, LORD,
   do I seek!   PSALM 27:8

**Glory to the Father,
and to the Son,
and to the Holy Spirit.**

Amen.

What is something in life that is a mystery to you?

Life has many mysteries. A mystery of faith is something we could not know unless God revealed it to us.

What do you already know about the mystery of who God is?

Celtic cross. The unbroken circle reminds us that God created us to be happy with him forever.

29

One God in Three Divine Persons

Faith Focus

How did the Church come to understand the mystery of the Holy Trinity?

Faith Vocabulary

Holy Trinity.
The central belief of the Christian faith; the mystery of one God in three divine Persons—God the Father, God the Son, God the Holy Spirit.

Annunciation.
The announcement to the Virgin Mary by the angel Gabriel that God had chosen her to be the mother of Jesus, the Son of God, through the power of the Holy Spirit.

The Holy Trinity

Jesus told his disciples, "Go, therefore, and make disciples of all nations, baptizing them in the name of the Father, and of the Son, and of the holy Spirit" (Matthew 28:19). The Church follows that command today.

Every time the Church baptizes a person, we name the mystery of who God is. We baptize in the name of the one God who is the **Holy Trinity.** The mystery of the Holy Trinity is the deepest and central belief of the Christian faith. This is a truth about God we could have never known unless God revealed it.

The Old Testament

In the Old Testament we read the beginning of the story of God's revelation of himself. This story is filled with people of faith.

God first revealed himself at creation to Adam and Eve. God made an everlasting covenant with Noah and with all living beings. Years later God came to Abraham and Sarah and revealed that he alone is God. Abraham came to believe in and trust in one God. His descendants, the Israelites, shared their faith in the one true God through many generations.

Check (✔) the ways you express faith in the Holy Trinity.

- ☐ **Bless myself**
- ☐ **Pray the creeds of the Church**
- ☐ **Pray the Glory Prayer**
- ☐ _____
_____
_____
(another way)

Mary, the Mother of Jesus

Many centuries after Abraham, God invited the Virgin Mary to place her trust in him. God chose the Virgin Mary to be the mother of Jesus, the Son of God and the Savior he promised to send. She became the mother of Jesus through the power of the Holy Spirit.

This event recorded in the Gospel is known as the **Annunciation.** It gives us a glimpse into the mystery of the Trinity. God chose Mary to be the mother of Jesus, the Son of God. So special is Mary's role in God's plan that she was free from all sin, from the very first moment of her conception, or existence, and throughout her whole life. We call this Mary's Immaculate Conception.

Jesus Christ

Throughout his life on earth, Jesus, the Son of God, spoke clearly of the Father and the Holy Spirit. On one occasion he told Philip the Apostle and the other disciples:

"The Advocate, the holy Spirit that the Father will send in my name—he will teach you everything and remind you of all that [I] told you."
JOHN 14:26

Christians have come to believe and understand that Jesus was speaking of one God, who is Father, Son, and Holy Spirit. Many years after the return of Jesus to his Father in heaven, the Church named this central mystery of our faith the Holy Trinity.

What did we come to know about God through Abraham, Mary, and Jesus?

Abraham	Mary	Jesus

Council of Nicaea, 325. Cesare Nebbia (1534–1614), Italian painter.

The Nicene Creed

Under the guidance of the Holy Spirit, two early councils of the Church taught about this great mystery of the Holy Trinity. These were the Council of Nicaea in A.D. 325 and the Council of Constantinople in A.D. 381. The Nicene Creed, which we profess at Mass, comes from these two councils.

We can never fully understand the mystery of the Holy Trinity. When our life on earth is completed, we will live forever with God in heaven. We will see God in a way we have never seen or known him before.

Use each letter in the word TRINITY. Write a word that tells something about the Trinity. Use the words to summarize what the Catholic Church teaches about the Trinity.

T
R
I
N
I
T
Y

Legend of Saint Augustine

Many Christians have tried to understand the mystery of the Holy Trinity. You may remember reading about Saint Augustine in chapter 1. There is a famous legend about him and his efforts to learn more about God.

One day Augustine was walking on the beach. The vast ocean inspired him to think about God. As he was walking along, he met a young boy who was taking water from the sea with a small bucket. Augustine watched as the boy kept pouring the water, one bucket at a time, into a hole he had dug in the sand.

Augustine became very curious and asked, "Why do you keep pouring water into the hole?" The boy answered, "Isn't it plain to see? I'm putting this ocean in the hole."

Augustine began to laugh. "That's impossible," he told the boy. "The great sea is way too large for that small hole." With loving eyes, the boy looked up and said, "And God is too big for your little mind." Suddenly, the boy disappeared.

Little by little with the guidance of the Holy Spirit, we can come to know the mystery of God the Holy Trinity in whose image we have been created.

What lesson did Saint Augustine learn? How can that lesson help you come to grow in your faith in God?

Our Catholic Identity

Holy Water

Blessing ourselves with holy water and saying, "In the name of the Father, and of the Son, and of the Holy Spirit" is a sacramental of the Church. Each time we bless ourselves, we remember our Baptism and profess our faith in the Holy Trinity.

What Difference Does Faith Make in My Life?

You believe there is one God in three Persons, God the Father, Son, and Holy Spirit. Little by little the Holy Spirit helps you understand this wonderful mystery about God.

Many people have helped you grow in your knowledge and love of the Holy Trinity. In the space below write one way you show your love for God the Father, God the Son, and God the Holy Spirit.

The Mystery of God

God the Father _____

_____ .

Jesus, the Son of God _____

_____ .

The Holy Spirit _____

_____ .

My Faith Choice

This week I will profess my faith in the Trinity. I will _____

_____ .

We Pray

Renewal of Faith

At Baptism we profess our faith in the Trinity. Each year at Easter the baptized renew the faith they professed at Baptism.

Leader: Do you believe in God, the Father Almighty?
All: **I do.**

Leader: Do you believe in Jesus Christ, his only Son our Lord?
All: **I do.**

Leader: Do you believe in the Holy Spirit?
All: **I do.**

We Remember

Circle whether each statement is true or false.

1. The Holy Spirit is the mystery of one God in three divine Persons.

   True   False

2. The Gospel account of the Annunciation tells us about God the Father, God the Son, and God the Holy Spirit.

   True   False

3. Jesus never spoke to his disciples about the Holy Spirit.

   True   False

To Help You Remember

1. The Holy Trinity is the central belief of the faith of the Church.

2. The mystery of the Trinity was most fully revealed in Jesus Christ.

3. We profess our belief in the Holy Trinity when we pray the Nicene Creed at Mass.

This Week . . .

In chapter 3, "The Mystery of the Holy Trinity," your child learned more about the Holy Trinity. The Holy Trinity is the mystery of one God in three Persons—God the Father, God the Son, and God the Holy Spirit. The mystery of God the Holy Trinity is the central mystery of the Christian faith. It is a truth about God that we could never have known unless God revealed it. God revealed this mystery over a long period of time. We profess faith in the Trinity at Baptism. Each time we pray the Nicene Creed at Mass we renew and profess our faith in this great mystery.

For more on the teachings of the Catholic Church on the mystery of the Holy Trinity, see *Catechism of the Catholic Church* paragraph numbers 232–260.

Sharing God's Word

Read together Matthew 28:16–20, the Gospel account of Jesus commissioning the disciples. Emphasize that we profess our faith in the Holy Trinity and remember our Baptism when we pray the Sign of the Cross.

Praying

In this chapter your child prayed a prayer renewing their baptismal promises. Read and pray together this prayer on page 35.

Making a Difference

Choose one of the following activities to do as a family or design a similar activity of your own.

- When we pray the Nicene Creed, we profess our faith in the Holy Trinity. Make Nicene Creed puzzles to help you memorize this important prayer of the Church. Write the Nicene Creed on a piece of paper. Cut the paper into small pieces. When you assemble the pieces, you will become more familiar with this creed.

- This week when your family takes part in Mass be sure to bless yourself with holy water as you enter and leave the church. Pray the Sign of the Cross and remember that you were baptized with water "in the name of the Father, and of the Son, and of the Holy Spirit."

- Talk about how your family is an image of the Holy Trinity. Name ways that your actions and words are signs of your love for one another.

For more ideas on ways your family can live your faith, visit the "Faith First for Families" page at **www.FaithFirst.com**. This week pay special attention to "Questions Kids Ask."

The Calming of the Sea
A Scripture Story

The Calming of the Storm at Sea, stained glass

We Pray

Trust in the LORD and do good
that you may dwell in the land and live secure. PSALM 37:3

Father, send the Holy Spirit to guide us and strengthen our faith.
Amen.

What sign of God's love for you have you seen today?

Signs of God's love for us are all around us. Jesus was the greatest sign of God's presence among us. Jesus performed many miracles to invite people to believe in God.

What are some of the Gospel accounts you know that tell about Jesus performing miracles?

Faith Focus

What does the story of Jesus calming the sea tell us about God?

Faith Vocabulary

public ministry of Jesus. The work that God the Father sent Jesus, the Son of God, to do on earth with the help of the Holy Spirit.

miracle. An action that goes beyond the laws of nature and invites us to deepen our faith in God.

The Sea of Galilee, noted for its severe and sudden storms

Jesus' Public Ministry

The **public ministry of Jesus** was the work the Father sent him to do with the help of the Holy Spirit. Most of that ministry took place in Galilee. Galilee was a section, or province, of the land of Palestine. It was there that Jesus began his preaching and first called people to be his disciples.

The Sea of Galilee is a large lake that is one of the most beautiful sights in Galilee. Without warning, storms often rise up and rage over it. Jesus visited the Sea of Galilee many times, and many Gospel stories take place near or on it.

Many of the first disciples of Jesus were fishermen who lived in Galilee and fished the Sea of Galilee. So Jesus used examples from the daily lives of his disciples to help them grow in faith and trust in God. He spoke of water and fish, wheat and lilies blooming in the fields of Galilee, and sheep and shepherds. All these examples helped his disciples and other people come to understand his teaching.

Look at the map on this page. What do you know about the two towns in Galilee?

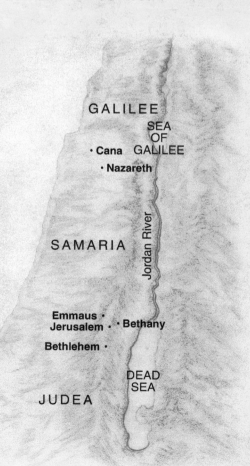

Jesus Calms the Sea

Here is one story about Jesus and the Sea of Galilee. It takes place in the evening.

After Jesus had spent the whole day teaching, he told his disciples that he would like to cross the Sea of Galilee. They got into a boat and as they were crossing, Jesus soon fell asleep.

A violent squall came up and waves were breaking over the boat, so that it was already filling up. Jesus was in the stern, asleep on a cushion. [The disciples] woke him and said to him, "Teacher, do you not care that we are perishing?" He woke up, rebuked the wind, and said to the sea, "Quiet! Be still!" The wind ceased and there was great calm. Then he asked them, "Why are you terrified? Do you not yet have faith?" They were filled with great awe and said to one another, "Who then is this whom even wind and sea obey?"

MARK 4:37–41

After this the disciples came to believe and trust in Jesus more and more. The more the disciples watched and listened to him, the stronger their faith and trust in God became.

Imagine that you interviewed the disciples after the boat landed. Write what the disciples learned from Jesus.

_____

_____

_____

_____

Jesus Works Signs and Wonders

On that dark stormy night, as the disciples were in the boat on the raging waters of the Sea of Galilee, they became terrified. Reaching the back of the boat, they woke Jesus, pleading, "Teacher, do you not care that we are perishing?" Jesus responded by calming the howling winds and stormy waters.

The Bible calls actions like this "mighty deeds, wonders, and signs" (Acts of the Apostles 2:22). We also call what happened on the Sea of Galilee a **miracle**. A miracle is an action that goes beyond the laws of nature and invites us to deepen our faith in God. We cannot fully explain a miracle, for it goes beyond what any of us can do on our own.

Miracles are important in the Bible because they are signs that remind us of God's mighty power and loving presence in our lives. When Jesus performed miracles, he was inviting the disciples (and us) to believe and trust in God's everlasting love and concern for us. The miracles of Jesus are also signs that the Father sent him. They invited people to believe in Jesus.

The storm in this story symbolizes all the frightening storms in our lives. This Gospel story tells us we are not alone during those moments. God, who loves us and cares for us, is always with us.

One form of prayer is called a prayer of meditation. Use these steps and meditate on the Gospel story of Jesus calming the storm.

- Think about a time when you experienced something that could be compared to "a frightening storm" in your life.

- Now think about Jesus calming the storm in the Scripture story you just read.

- Compare the meaning of this Gospel story to your own "frightening storm" experience.

- What did you learn from this reflection?

_____

_____

_____

Our Church Makes a Difference

Catholic Relief Services distributing food at a mother/baby clinic in a village near Bembereke, Benin, West Africa

Catholic Relief Services

The Church is a sign of the loving presence of God in the world. In 1943 the Catholic bishops of the United States founded Catholic Relief Services to give witness to that presence through service to people in need.

The people of Catholic Relief Services preach the Gospel by their actions. With the help and guidance of the Holy Spirit, they live the Gospel among people who are suffering and they announce the Gospel of love and justice proclaimed by Jesus.

When people are suffering from poverty, Catholic Relief Services is there assisting them and helping them find ways to better their lives. When people are suffering from natural disasters, such as earthquakes and floods, Catholic Relief Services is there. When people are suffering from man-made disasters, such as war, Catholic Relief Services is there helping people rebuild their communities.

Today the people of Catholic Relief Services are present in more than eighty countries. Like Jesus, they invite people by their words and actions to deepen their faith and trust in God.

What other ways do you see the Church living as a sign of God's caring love in the world?

Young boy waiting to receive food in the Catholic Relief Services camp in Bujumbura, Burundi, Central Africa

What Difference Does Faith Make in My Life?

The Holy Spirit helps the Church live as a sign of God's love. Through your kindness to people, God invites others to believe and trust in him.

Symbol of Trust and Faith in Jesus Christ

Design a symbol that reminds you of Jesus and his great love for you. Use your symbol to remember to place your trust in Jesus.

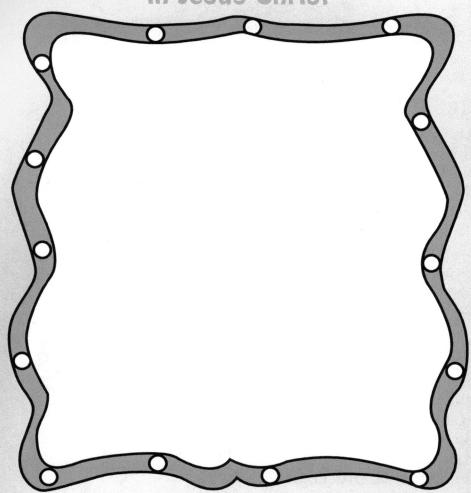

 My Faith Choice

This week I will remember how much Jesus loves me and I will place my trust in him. I will do this by

_____

_____.

Lord, In You We Trust

The Book of Psalms is the inspired word of God. When we pray the Psalms, the Holy Spirit inspires us and teaches us to pray.

All: **God is our refuge and our strength.**

Group 1:   In times of trouble,
Group 2:   LORD, in you I place my trust.

Group 1:   When the earth shakes and waters roar,
Group 2:   LORD, in you I place my trust.

Group 1:   When nations rage in war,
Group 2:   LORD, in you I place my trust.

All: **God is our refuge and our strength.**
                            BASED ON PSALM 46:2–4, 7–8

We Remember

Circle the words hidden in the puzzle. Use each word in a sentence and share its meaning with a partner.

```
F  B  D  G  A  L  I  L  E  E  L
H  M  I  N  I  S  T  R  Y  S  W
T  Y  M  I  R  A  C  L  E  P  T
R  G  T  R  U  S  T  T  I  G  K
T  Y  V  B  E  L  I  E  V  E  H
```

To Help You Remember

1. The public ministry of Jesus is the work the Father sent him to do with the help of the Holy Spirit.

2. Jesus' calming the storm on the Sea of Galilee was one of the miracle stories in the Gospel.

3. Jesus performed miracles to invite people to believe and trust in God.

With My Family

This Week . . .

In chapter 4, "The Calming of the Sea: A Scripture Story," your child listened to and reflected on the miracle of Jesus calming the Sea of Galilee. Much of the ministry of Jesus that is recorded in the Gospels takes place in Galilee. This Gospel story is one of the many miracle stories that are part of Jesus' ministry. The miracles of Jesus were signs and wonders pointing to the saving presence of God in the world. They were invitations to deepen one's faith and trust in God and to believe in Jesus, the Son of God, sent by the Father.

For more on the teachings of the Catholic Church on the public ministry of Jesus, see *Catechism of the Catholic Church* paragraph numbers 534–560.

Sharing God's Word

Read together the Gospel account in Mark 4:35–41 about Jesus calming the storm. Emphasize that Jesus taught the disciples to believe and trust in God.

Praying

In this chapter your child prayed a prayer of trust based on Psalm 46. Read and pray together this prayer on page 43.

Making a Difference

Choose one of the following activities to do as a family or design a similar activity of your own.

- Pretend that you were one of the disciples in the boat with Jesus. Share what you would tell people when you got back to shore.

- Make an Ichthus (the Christian fish symbol). Display the symbol where it can serve as a reminder of your faith in Jesus Christ, Son of God and Savior of the world.

- Talk about how your family shows that you trust in Jesus' love for you. Decide some ways that, as a family, you can invite others to believe and trust in Jesus.

For more ideas on ways your family can live your faith, visit the "Faith First for Families" page at **www.FaithFirst.com**. Take time to read an article from "Just for Parents" this week.

Great Is the Lord, Our God

We Pray

Sing to the LORD a
    new song;
  sing to the LORD,
    all the earth. PSALM 96:1

Blessed are you,
Lord, God
of all creation.   Amen.

*What is an image you
would use to describe
yourself?*

We use images to describe
the qualities of people.
For example, we might
say, "She's as fast as
lightning." Look at the
world. Creation helps us
come to know God.

*What image from God's
creation tells something
about God's goodness?*

Faith Focus

Who has God revealed himself to be?

Faith Vocabulary

attributes of God. Qualities of God that help us understand the mystery of God.

Abba. The name Jesus used for God the Father that reveals the love and trust that exist between Jesus, God the Son, and God the Father.

Attributes of God

God is a God of wonder and awe who has revealed himself. To help us understand who God has revealed himself to be, the inspired writers of the Bible have used certain qualities to describe him. These qualities are called **attributes of God**. Out of great and everlasting love, God has created us and revealed himself. God wants us to know, trust, and love him. Here are a few of the attributes God has revealed about himself.

One

God is one. There is only one God. There is no one and nothing like him.

> Hear, O Israel! The LORD is our God, the LORD alone! DEUTERONOMY 6:4

Lord

God revealed the name *YHWH* to describe himself. The writers of the Bible used the name *Adonai*, or Lord, in place of the divine and sacred name *YHWH*.

Almighty

God is almighty. This means that God alone can do anything.

> May God Almighty bless you . . . that you may become an assembly of peoples. GENESIS 28:3

Eternal

God is eternal. God always has been and always will be. God had no beginning and will have no end.

> The LORD is the eternal God. ISAIAH 40:28

Holy

God is holy. The word *holy* means "set apart." No one and no thing that God created is equal to him.

> "Holy, holy, holy is the LORD of hosts!" ISAIAH 6:3

Love

God is love. God created and saved us to share in that love.

> "God is love." 1 JOHN 4:16

Truth

God is truth. God is always faithful to his word. He always keeps his promises.

> The LORD's word is true. PSALM 33:4

What is your favorite attribute of God? Tell a partner why it is your favorite attribute.

God the Father

God has revealed himself most fully in Jesus Christ. Jesus spoke about God in many ways. Most of all Jesus spoke about God the Father.

Jesus had a very special name for God. He called God **Abba,** which means "dear Father" or even "dad." When people used the name Abba, they showed how close they were to their father and how much they loved and trusted him. When Jesus called God Abba, he revealed how much he loved and trusted his Father.

Jesus invited his disciples to love and trust God the Father as he did. He said, "This is how you are to pray:

Our Father . . ."
MATTHEW 6:9

Jesus revealed that his Father is our Father too. God the Father loves us and knows each of us by name. We are his children. When we call God Father, we are saying that we are all children of God. We believe and trust and love God our Abba, our Father.

Write and decorate your favorite name for God. Use that name today to tell others about him. Pray it often.

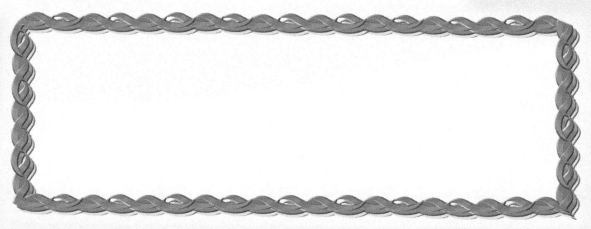

God the Creator

Creation shows the great glory of God. God created the whole universe and all creatures, seen and unseen, out of nothing and without any help. Everyone and everything God created is good.

God created people in his image and likeness. He created us with a body and a spiritual and immortal soul. This means our soul will never die.

The writers of the Bible gave the names Adam and Eve to the first humans. No matter the color of our skin, the life we live, the language we speak, we all belong to one family—the family of God.

Original Sin

Sadly, Adam and Eve were not satisfied with God's plan of goodness and holiness for them. They preferred their own way to God's plan and disobeyed God. The Church calls their decision to live apart from God original sin. It is called original sin because it is the beginning of all evil and sin in the world.

Original sin wounded everyone and everything God created. Each person is born sharing in the effects of original sin, and there is evil in the world. Despite original sin, God still invites and helps everyone to share in his goodness and love. He sent Jesus, his only Son, to redeem us and restore our friendship with God.

Illustrate one way you can show your respect for God and give him honor and glory.

Glory to God

Our Church Makes a Difference

Blessing Prayers

Blessings are one of the ways the Church shows that we believe God the Creator is always with his creation. He is always blessing us with his love. Blessing prayers remind us of this important truth about God.

Catholics use many blessing prayers. We pray grace before and after meals. At the conclusion of Mass, we ask God to bless us.

We ask God's blessing on every newly married couple. Some people ask for a blessing when they move into a new home or before they go off to college. Catholics also bless religious objects such as medals, rosaries, and crucifixes.

All our blessings remind us that God, who knows and loves each of us by name, is always with us. This is the greatest good and blessing we ever could have.

Describe why blessing a person, place, or object is a sign of faith.

Sacramentals

Blessings of people, meals, objects, and places are sacramentals. Sacramentals are sacred signs given to us by the Church. Some blessings consecrate people, objects, or places to God. Blessings are the most important sacramentals of the Church.

What Difference Does Faith Make in My Life?

You show that you believe in and trust in God the Father, as Jesus did, in many ways. You pray. You treat others and the world with respect and kindness.

Imagine you are a movie director. You are directing a movie entitled All About God. In this space illustrate or write about a scene in that movie.

All About God

My Faith Choice

This week I will share my faith in God by making known one quality about him. I will

_____

_____.

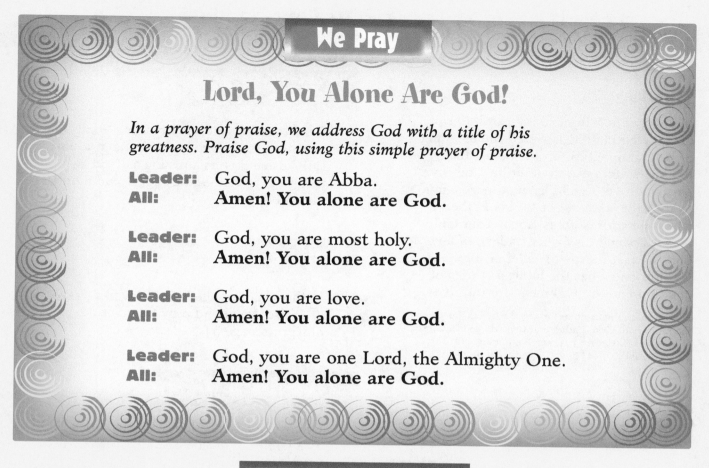

We Pray

Lord, You Alone Are God!

In a prayer of praise, we address God with a title of his greatness. Praise God, using this simple prayer of praise.

Leader: God, you are Abba.
All: **Amen! You alone are God.**

Leader: God, you are most holy.
All: **Amen! You alone are God.**

Leader: God, you are love.
All: **Amen! You alone are God.**

Leader: God, you are one Lord, the Almighty One.
All: **Amen! You alone are God.**

We Remember

Unscramble the letters of the words in the word box. Then match the words with their meanings.

teribusatt	**luso**	**naligori sni**

1. The qualities of God

_____

2. The spiritual dimension of the human person that never dies and lives forever

_____

3. The sin committed by Adam and Eve

_____

To Help You Remember

1. One, almighty, holy, eternal, love, and truth are qualities about himself that God has revealed.

2. God is the creator of everyone and everything, seen and unseen.

3. Adam and Eve disobeyed God and turned away from his goodness. This sin caused the beginning of all other sin in the world.

This Week . . .

In chapter 5, "Great Is the Lord, Our God," your child discovered the meaning of several qualities, or attributes, the biblical writers use to describe God. In particular, your child listened once again to Jesus' love and trust for his Father, whom he addressed as Abba. Your child also deepened his or her understanding of both what it means to call God the Creator and what the biblical stories of creation and the Fall mean for our lives.

For more on the teachings of the Catholic Church on the mystery of God, Father and Creator, see *Catechism of the Catholic Church* paragraph numbers 199–227, 268–274, and 279–412.

Sharing God's Word

Read together and quietly think about the Scripture verses on page 46 one at a time. Emphasize that as amazing as God is, Jesus taught us to call God a simple and familiar name, Father.

Praying

In this chapter your child prayed a prayer of praise. Read and pray together this prayer on page 51.

Making a Difference

Choose one of the following activities to do as a family or design a similar activity of your own.

- Choose one of the Scripture verses on page 46. Make a banner using the verse. Display the banner where it can remind everyone how wonderful God is.

- God created the entire universe. Choose one thing you can do to show your respect for God by respecting his creation.

- This Sunday when you take part in Mass, take time to look at the religious statues or artwork in your church. Talk about how these works of art help you honor and worship God.

For more ideas on ways your family can live your faith, visit the "Faith First for Families" page at **www.FaithFirst.com**. You will find the "Contemporary Issues" page helpful this week.

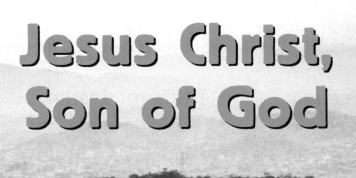

Jesus Christ, Son of God

We Pray

O LORD, our Lord, how awesome is your name through all the earth! PSALM 8:2

Lord, God our Father, may we who honor the holy name of Jesus, your Son, enjoy his friendship both in this life and in his kingdom forever.

Amen.

Why are people's names important to them?

Your name is very important. The angel told Joseph to name Mary's Son, Jesus.

What does the name Jesus mean?

Christ the Redeemer, Rio de Janeiro, Brazil

The Son of God and the Son of Mary

Faith Focus

Why is Jesus called both Son of God and Son of Mary?

Faith Vocabulary

Christ. A title for Jesus that states that he is the Messiah whom God promised to send to save his people.

Lord. A title for Jesus that states that Jesus is truly God.

The Name *Jesus*

In the Bible people's names often describe the roles they played in God's plan of salvation. In Matthew's Gospel we are told that an angel appeared to Joseph, telling him that Mary would give birth to a son and that he was to name the child Jesus. The Hebrew name *Jesus* means "God saves." The very name of Jesus reveals that he is the Savior of the world.

All of God's promises in the Bible come true in Jesus. Jesus is the center and heart of God's loving plan of creation and salvation. Jesus **Christ** is the Messiah, the **Lord** and Savior of the world.

Titles for Jesus

There are also several important names or titles for Jesus in the Gospels. These express our faith about who Jesus is and the work the Father sent him to do.

Messiah Throughout the Old Testament God promised to send a messiah. The title *messiah* means "anointed one." The messiah would be a king who would save, or deliver, God's people from their enemies.

Christ The English word *Christ* is used for the Hebrew word *messiah* and for the Greek word *kristos*. Jesus is the Christ—the Messiah or Anointed One.

Lord The Israelites used the word *Lord* for God in place of the name *YHWH*. When we call Jesus "Lord," we are professing our faith that Jesus Christ is truly God. He is the Son of God, the second divine Person of the Holy Trinity. Jesus is true God and true man.

Describe how all these above titles taken together help you come to know who Jesus is.

Visit of the Shepherds, stained glass

The Birth of Jesus

The announcement of the birth of Jesus was a special moment in the life of the Virgin Mary. The angel Gabriel brought Mary a message telling her that God had chosen her to be the mother of the Son of God. The Holy Spirit would come to the Virgin Mary, and she would conceive and give birth to a son and name him Jesus. We call this moment in the life of Mary the Annunciation.

After the birth of Jesus, Luke's Gospel tells us that an angel of God appeared to shepherds, proclaiming the good news of Jesus' birth. The angel said to them:

"[T]oday in the city of David a savior has been born for you who is Messiah and Lord."
LUKE 2:11

The Church names the mystery of the Son of God becoming man the Incarnation. The word *incarnation* means "putting on flesh." It is the word the Church has chosen to name our belief that the Son of God, the second Person of the Holy Trinity, became fully human without giving up being fully God. Jesus Christ is true God and true man.

Faith-Filled People

Matthew and Luke

Saint Matthew was a tax collector and an Apostle. Saint Luke was a physician and a companion of Saint Paul the Apostle. It is only in the Gospel of Matthew and in the Gospel of Luke that we read the account of the birth of Jesus.

Use words or pictures to describe what you can do to express your faith in Jesus Christ.

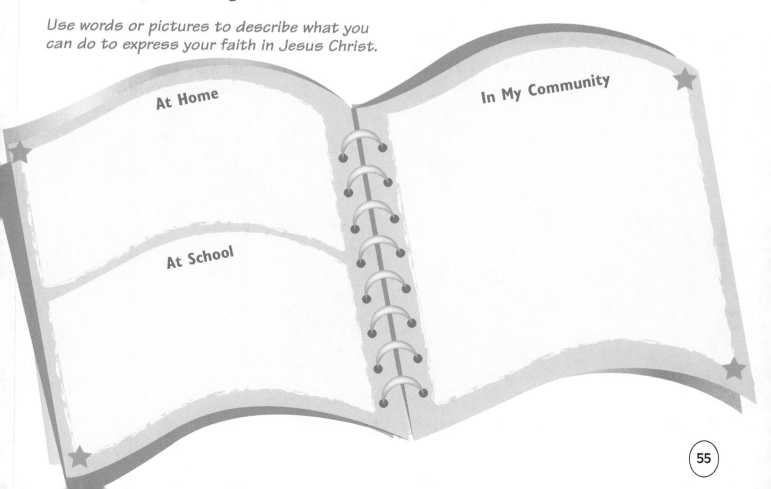

At Home

At School

In My Community

Mother of Jesus

The four Gospels do not tell us much about the life of Jesus as he grew up with Mary and Joseph. His life was probably very much like the life of other families who lived in Nazareth. Mary and Joseph shared the faith of the Jewish people with Jesus. They taught him the customs and practices of their religion.

The Gospels tell us that Mary sometimes traveled with Jesus and his disciples. She listened to him as he preached and taught. When he was crucified, Mary, several other women disciples, and John, the "disciple whom Jesus loved," were there with him.

Mother of God

Mary is truly the Mother of God because Jesus is true God and true man. We remember and celebrate this truth about Mary each year on January 1, the feast of Mary, the Mother of God.

Mary, Our Mother

Mary is our Blessed Mother. She is the Mother of the Church. Since the earliest days of the Church, Christians have looked upon Mary as our mother. We believe and trust that Mary cares for us, watches over us, and wants us to grow closer to her Son, Jesus.

Catholics honor Mary and show their devotion and love for her in many ways. In this space write how you can show Mary your love for her.

Mary, Our Mother

Our Church Makes a Difference

Madonna and Child

From the earliest days of the Church, Christian artists have proclaimed the Nativity, or the story of the birth of Jesus, through painting, sculpture, woodcarvings, and music. The Christian belief in Mary and her Son, Jesus, is often expressed through the portrayal of Mary holding the Christ child. These works of art are called "Madonna and Child." The word *Madonna* means "My Lady."

Look at the art of the "Madonna and Child." Share what they tell you about the faith of people in Mary and her Child.

Mosaic

Woodcarving

Marble sculpture

What Difference Does Faith Make in My Life?

Each year during Christmastime you celebrate the birth of Jesus. You celebrate God's love for you, for your family, and for all people. The Holy Spirit invites you to celebrate that love and share it with others each and every day.

Sharing the Good News

Create a banner. Use words, pictures, or symbols that tell others about Jesus Christ.

My Faith Choice

This week I will show others that I believe in Jesus Christ. I will

_____

_____.

We Pray

Praise the Name of the Lord

Pray this prayer of petition. Ask God to help you come to know and love him better.

Leader: Jesus, Son of the living God,
All: **have mercy on us.**

Leader: Jesus, Son of the Virgin Mary,
All: **have mercy on us.**

Leader: Jesus, the Good Shepherd,
All: **have mercy on us.**

We Remember

Choose the attribute of God or title of Jesus. Write it next to its meaning.

Messiah   Christ   Lord   Jesus

Meaning	Attributes
God Saves	_____
Anointed One	_____
Truly God	_____
Messiah	_____

To Help You Remember

1. Jesus Christ is the Messiah.

2. Jesus Christ is Lord. He is true God, the second Person of the Holy Trinity, who became true man without giving up being God.

3. The Virgin Mary is the mother of Jesus, the Son of God.

This Week . . .

In chapter 6, "Jesus Christ, Son of God," your child learned more about Jesus and the mystery of the Incarnation. The name *Jesus* means "God saves." It reveals to us that Jesus is truly the Savior of the world. Other names, or titles, for Jesus such as Christ, Lord, and Messiah help us understand who Jesus is and the work God the Father sent him to do. The mystery of the Son of God taking on flesh and becoming fully human is called the Incarnation. We believe that Jesus Christ is true God and true man. Mary, the Mother of Jesus, is truly the Mother of God because Jesus is true God and true man.

For more on the teachings of the Catholic Church on the mystery of the Incarnation, see *Catechism of the Catholic Church* paragraph numbers 422–451, 456–478, and 484–507.

Sharing God's Word

Read together the Bible story about the birth of Jesus at the beginning of the Gospel according to Matthew or the Gospel according to Luke. Emphasize what the Gospel account of Jesus' birth tells about who he is and the work he was sent to do.

Praying

In this chapter your child prayed a prayer of petition. Read and pray together this prayer on page 59.

Making a Difference

Choose one of the following activities to do as a family or design a similar activity of your own.

- The angel Gabriel told Mary to name her child Jesus. Names are very important. Talk about how each family member's name was chosen.

- Jesus showed his love for his mother. It is very important to show our love for family members. Be sure to do special things this week to show your love for one another.

- Saint Nicholas is the patron saint of children. Find out more about this generous saint. Look in your local library, parish library, or on the Internet by visiting *The Catholic Encyclopedia* Web site.

For more ideas on ways your family can live your faith, visit the "Faith First for Families" page at **www.FaithFirst.com**. This week share some of the ideas with one another on the "Gospel Reflections" page.

7

The Death, Resurrection, and Ascension of Jesus

We Pray

This is the day the LORD
  has made;
let us rejoice in it
  and be glad.

PSALM 118:24

**God our Father,
you raised Christ
your Son from the dead.
Raise us to new life
in Christ by the Holy
Spirit who is within us.**
       Amen.

*What are some of the key
events in the life of your
family?*

Every person's life has
key events. Each time we
celebrate the Eucharist
we remember the Paschal
Mystery of the Passion,
death, Resurrection, and
glorious Ascension of
Jesus Christ.

*What do you know about
the Passion, death,
Resurrection, and Ascension
of Jesus?*

Jesus. Oil on wood. Daniel
Nevins, contemporary
American painter.

The Paschal Mystery of Jesus

How does the Jewish feast of Passover help us understand the Paschal Mystery of Jesus?

Faith Vocabulary

Passover. The Jewish feast celebrating the sparing of the Hebrew children from death and the passage of God's people from slavery in Egypt to freedom in the land God promised them.

Paschal Mystery. The "passing over" of Jesus from life through death into new and glorious life; the Passion, death, Resurrection, and glorious Ascension of Jesus.

Jewish family celebrating Passover

Passover

One of the most important events in the history of the Israelites, or Hebrews, was God's freeing them from slavery in Egypt. God had entered a covenant with Abraham, blessing and choosing him to be the father of God's people. When God's people were suffering from a great famine, Abraham's descendants traveled to Egypt in search of food. Joseph, Abraham's great-grandson, was already living there and was a highly respected leader in Egypt. He recognized his family, fed them, and invited them to stay in Egypt.

Over a period of time, the Egyptians made the Hebrews their slaves. God's people prayed, asking God to deliver, or free, them from slavery.

God chose and sent Moses to lead his people to freedom. Moses and his brother Aaron bravely faced Pharaoh, the Egyptian king. Over and over they tried to persuade Pharaoh to let the Hebrews leave Egypt.

Again and again Pharaoh refused despite the signs that God sent. Then something happened. Many young Egyptians were dying in their homes, but the Hebrews and their children were being spared. Death "passed over" the homes of the Hebrews.

Finally, Pharaoh let God's people go. The Jewish people gather each year in the springtime to remember and celebrate what happened. They call the celebration **Passover.**

How can faith in God help a person deal with suffering?

The Paschal Mystery

The Passion, death, Resurrection, and glorious Ascension of Jesus is called the **Paschal Mystery**. It is the passing over of Jesus from life through death into a new and glorious life. It is the most important event in Jesus' life, and the central theme of the Gospel.

The Passion Narrative

The part of the Gospel that tells about Jesus' suffering and death is called the Passion narrative.

The Last Supper. During the week in which Jesus died, he went to Jerusalem and celebrated Passover. At a Passover meal with his disciples, which Christians have named the Last Supper, Jesus gave the Church the Eucharist.

The Betrayal and Arrest. After the Last Supper, Judas led a group of enemies to the Garden of Gethsemane where Jesus was praying. It was there Judas betrayed Jesus and handed him over to be arrested.

The Trial and Sentencing. Accusing him of blasphemy, Jesus' enemies handed him over to Pilate to be tried. Fearing the Roman emperor and the crowd, Pilate handed Jesus over to be crucified.

Suffering, Death, and Burial. Jesus carried his cross to Calvary, a hill outside Jerusalem where criminals were crucified. It was there that Jesus died. After Jesus died, Joseph of Arimathea and other disciples of Jesus buried his body in a new tomb.

Faith-Filled People

Veronica

The Church passes on to us the tradition that as Jesus was carrying his cross he was met by Veronica, one of his disciples. Veronica reached out and wiped the blood and sweat off Jesus' face with her veil. This act of faith and compassion is remembered in the Sixth Station of the Way of the Cross. The Church celebrates the feast day of Saint Veronica on July 9.

Imagine you are with the disciples at Jesus' arrest and trial. On this journal page describe your thoughts and feelings.

The Resurrection

Three days after Jesus died and was buried, he was raised to new life. We call this mighty deed of God the Resurrection. It is the heart of our Christian faith. When we say that Jesus was raised from the dead, we do not mean he simply came back to life. While the Risen Christ appeared to his disciples in the body they knew, they at first did not recognize him because his body was gloriously changed by the Holy Spirit. God raised Jesus into a new and glorious life.

The Ascension

For forty days after the Resurrection, the Risen Jesus met with his disciples and continued to teach them. During one final meeting on the Mount of Olives, which is near Jerusalem, he ascended to his Father. We call this the Ascension.

When we say we believe in the Ascension, we mean:

- Jesus has returned in glory and majesty to his Father.
- Jesus has gone to prepare a place for us. Where Christ has ascended, we hope one day to follow.
- We are responsible for continuing the mission of Jesus on earth.

Through his Paschal Mystery, Jesus frees us from sin. Raised to new life by the power of the Holy Spirit, Christ shares with us the fullness of life with God. With Christ, we can "pass over" from sin and death to new life with him, his Father, and the Holy Spirit. God's plan of salvation is fulfilled in Jesus Christ.

Draw a sign or symbol that illustrates the faith of Catholics in the Paschal Mystery.

Our Church Makes a Difference

Interior of Church of the Holy Sepulchre, Jerusalem, site of the Tenth Station through the Fourteenth Station

Our Catholic Identity

Pilgrimage

A pilgrimage is a journey to a sacred place or shrine. Each year many Christians make a pilgrimage to Jerusalem to travel Jesus' final journey through the streets of Jerusalem to his Crucifixion on Calvary.

Stations of the Cross

Ever since the early centuries of Christianity, people have made pilgrimages to the Holy Land to visit the places associated with the life, death, and Resurrection of Jesus Christ. Because not everyone could visit the Holy Land, shrines to commemorate the Passion and death of Christ were placed in churches throughout the world. These shrines became known as the Stations, or Way, of the Cross.

When we make our pilgrimage and pray the Stations of the Cross, we share our belief in the Paschal Mystery and announce that God's plan of salvation is fulfilled in Christ. By his death Jesus has conquered death and won life everlasting for all people.

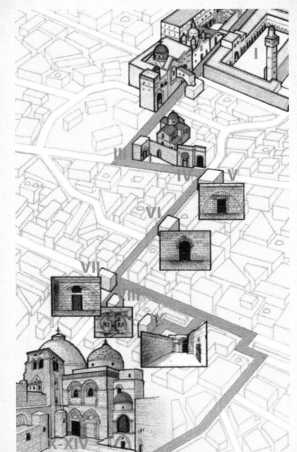

As you pray the Stations, what might you say to Jesus to express your love for him?

Actual Stations of the Cross, Jerusalem

What Difference Does Faith Make in My Life?

Through Baptism you were made a sharer in the death and Resurrection of Christ. You received the gift of the Holy Spirit and the promise and hope of eternal life.

We are Easter people. We share joy and hope with people who are sad. We share love where there is hatred. In this space create a symbol or design a banner that announces the good news of Jesus' Resurrection.

My Faith Choice

This week I will share my faith in the Risen Christ with others. I will

_____

_____.

We Pray

Rejoice! Rejoice!

The Easter Vigil is the Church's great celebration of the Resurrection. At the Easter Vigil the Exsultet *is sung. The* Exsultet *is a joyful proclamation announcing the Resurrection of Jesus and the gift of hope to the world. Pray together the beginning of this prayer.*

Group 1: Exult, let them exult, the hosts of heaven, exult, let Angel ministers of God exult,

Group 2: let the trumpet of salvation sound aloud our mighty King's triumph!

Group 1: Be glad, let earth be glad as glory floods her, ablaze with light from her eternal King,

Group 2: let all corners of the earth be glad, knowing an end to gloom and darkness.

All: **Alleluia! Sound the trumpet of salvation!**

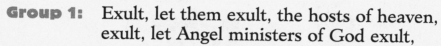

We Remember

Use the clues to discover the events and meaning of the Paschal Mystery.

ACROSS

3. The ___ Supper is the Passover meal Jesus celebrated with his disciples.

4. We call Jesus being raised from the dead the ___.

DOWN

1. Forty days after Easter we celebrate the ___.

2. Jesus was crucified on a hill called ___.

To Help You Remember

1. The Passover is the feast the Jewish people celebrate to remember God's freeing them from slavery in Egypt and leading them to a new life in the land he had promised them.

2. The Paschal Mystery of Jesus is his Passion, death, Resurrection, and glorious Ascension.

3. By his Paschal Mystery Christ freed people from death and sin and gained for all the promise and hope of eternal life.

Grade 5 • Chapter 7   67

This Week . . .

In chapter 7, "The Death, Resurrection, and Ascension of Jesus," your child deepened their faith in the Passion, death, Resurrection, and glorious Ascension of Jesus. During the week in which he died, Jesus celebrated a Passover meal with his disciples. Passover is the Jewish feast that celebrates the passage of God's people from slavery in Egypt to freedom. The Paschal Mystery of Jesus is his Passion, death, Resurrection, and glorious Ascension—his passover from suffering and death to new and glorious life.

For more on the teachings of the Catholic Church on the Paschal Mystery of Christ, see *Catechism of the Catholic Church* paragraph numbers 571–664.

Sharing God's Word

Invite each person to share what they know about the Gospel accounts of Jesus' Passion, death, Resurrection, and Ascension. Emphasize that each time we celebrate the Eucharist, we are made sharers in the Paschal Mystery.

Praying

In this chapter your child prayed the *Exultet*. Read and pray together this prayer on page 67.

Making a Difference

Choose one of the following activities to do as a family or design a similar activity of your own.

- At Mass we celebrate the Paschal Mystery. When you take part in Mass this week, look for the crucifix and the Paschal candle. Talk about how these remind you of the Paschal Mystery.

- Imagine that you were present with the disciples when Jesus was arrested and put on trial. Talk about how you would have felt or what you would have thought.

- This week when you take part in Mass, spend time afterward walking the Stations of the Cross. Stop at each station and talk about what each station tells about Jesus' Passion and death.

For more ideas on ways your family can live your faith, visit the "Faith First for Families" page at **www.FaithFirst.com**. Click on "Family Prayer" to find a special prayer to pray together this week.

ff

The Promise of a Helper
A Scripture Story

8

Descent of Holy Spirit upon the Disciples, stained glass

We Pray

I wait for you,
    O LORD; . . .
In you I trust.   PSALM 25:1, 2

Father,
we turn to you
in all our troubles.
We give you thanks
in all our joys.   Amen.

What kinds of promises do people make to each other?

Promises are important. The Bible passes on to us story after story of God keeping his promises to people.

What are some of God's promises?

Bible Background

How does the Holy Spirit help us and the Church share our faith in Jesus?

Faith Vocabulary

Evangelists. The writers of the four Gospels in the New Testament—Matthew, Mark, Luke, and John.

The New Testament

After Jesus' Ascension, the Apostles and other disciples first spoke to others about Jesus. This is called oral tradition. Then the Church, inspired by the Holy Spirit, began to write down the teachings of the Apostles about Jesus and the importance of the meaning of his life and teachings for all people. The New Testament is the collection of these writings.

Inspired by the Holy Spirit, the **Evangelists** Matthew, Mark, Luke, and John each wrote an account of the Gospel. Each of these written Gospels passes on the faith of the Church in Jesus Christ. They announce the good news of God's saving love.

John's Gospel is the fourth Gospel in the New Testament. It was written toward the end of the first century when Christians were being persecuted and martyred, or put to death because of their faith in Jesus Christ.

Share your faith in Jesus Christ. Create a Web page of pictures and phrases that tell others about him.

Sharing the Good News

Last Supper Discourse,
stained glass

Jesus' Promise

At the Last Supper, Jesus spoke to his disciples about many things. He told them he would soon be leaving them and returning to his Father. He taught them to love each other as he had loved them. Jesus also made this promise.

"But now I am going to the one who sent me, and not one of you asks me, 'Where are you going?' But because I told you this, grief has filled your hearts. But I tell you the truth, it is better for you that I go. For if I do not go, the Advocate will not come to you. But if I go, I will send him to you."

JOHN 16:5–7

The disciples listened to Jesus. But they did not fully understand what he was saying. While they were frightened and confused that he would soon leave them and return to his Father, they trusted that the Advocate promised by Jesus would come to them.

When do you pray to the Holy Spirit?

The Holy Spirit is always at work in the Church. He is the Teacher who helps the Church understand what Jesus taught. The Holy Spirit is the Advocate who gives the Church the gifts necessary to live Jesus' command to love one another as he did.

As Christians we pray for the grace to open our hearts and minds to the Holy Spirit. Praying to the Holy Spirit makes all the difference in the way we live each day.

Complete this prayer. Make it your own personal prayer. Keep a copy of your prayer in your Bible or some other place. Pray it each day.

The Advocate

The Holy Spirit is the Advocate whom Jesus promised would come. An advocate is one who speaks up for someone. The Holy Spirit is always with us and gives us strength for all the hard times in our lives. He gives us the grace to live with courage and confidence. The Holy Spirit never leaves us alone.

Come, Holy Spirit,

_____

_____

_____

_____

_____

_____

_____

_____

_____

_____.

Our Church Makes a Difference

Hymns

From the earliest days of the Church, Christians have lifted up their hearts and minds in prayer to God in song. Hymns are one form of song that has long been a part of the prayer tradition of the Church.

Some hymns are found in the New Testament. Other hymns have been composed recently. Many of the hymns we sing as a faith community are found in your parish hymnal. The words of the hymns express the Church's faith. There are hymns about God the Father and Creator. Other hymns profess our faith in Jesus and the saving events of his life.

This hymn to the Holy Spirit was written in the ninth century:

Come, Holy Spirit,
Creator blest,
And in our hearts
take up thy rest;
Come with thy grace
and heavenly aid
To fill the hearts
which thou hast made.

There are other hymns about Mary and the other saints. There are hymns that help us celebrate the liturgical seasons. Singing hymns is one way we profess the faith of the Church and proclaim it to others.

Our Catholic Identity

The Magnificat

The Magnificat is a canticle, or sacred song, found in Luke's Gospel. The Church prays or sings the Magnificat each day. It is prayed as part of the Evening Prayer of the Liturgy of the Hours. The Liturgy of the Hours is the liturgical, daily, public, communal prayer of the Church.

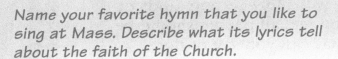

Name your favorite hymn that you like to sing at Mass. Describe what its lyrics tell about the faith of the Church.

What Difference Does Faith Make in My Life?

The Holy Spirit is always by your side. He is your advocate and teacher, guiding you to be a person of faith and hope and love.

Choose one of these two situations. Then write what the Holy Spirit can help you do or say in that situation.

Come, Holy Spirit

1. The city or town where you live does not want a homeless shelter for people who are poor. What can you say or do to help?

   _____

   _____

   _____

   _____

2. A group you belong to only will allow certain kinds of people to join the group. You feel all people should be allowed to be members. What can you say or do?

   _____

   _____

   _____

   _____

My Faith Choice

I will remember that the Holy Spirit is always with me. When I am faced with a difficult choice to live my faith, I will

_____

_____.

Prayer to the Holy Spirit

On Pentecost the Church prays aloud or sings the prayer, "Veni, Sancte Spiritus," or "Come, Holy Spirit." Pray this part of the prayer. Use prayer gestures as you pray.

Holy Spirit, Lord Divine,
Come, from heights of heav'n and shine,
** Come with blessed radiance bright!**
Come, O Father of the poor,
Come, whose treasured Gifts endure,
** Come, our heart's unfailing light!**

We Remember

Decode the faith message.

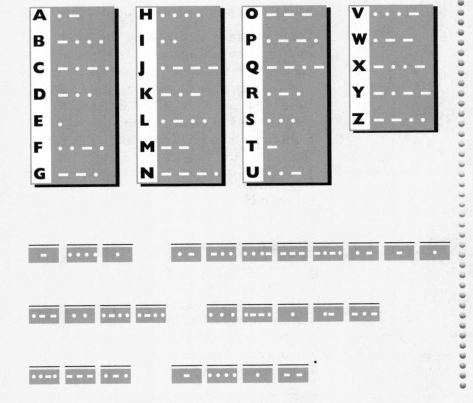

To Help You Remember

1. Jesus promised that he would not leave his disciples alone after he returned to his Father.

2. Jesus promised that the Advocate would come to the disciples.

3. The Holy Spirit is the Advocate who Jesus promised would always be with the disciples and the Church.

This Week . . .

In chapter 8, "The Promise of a Helper: A Scripture Story," your child deepened their understanding of the Gospel, the announcement of the Good News of salvation in Jesus Christ. The four writers of the Gospel—Matthew, Mark, Luke, and John—are called the Evangelists. The Gospel according to John, also known as the Fourth Gospel, records that at the Last Supper, Jesus promised that the Holy Spirit would always be with the Church as her advocate and teacher.

For more on the teachings of the Catholic Church on the mystery of the Holy Spirit, see *Catechism of the Catholic Church* paragraph numbers 683–741.

Sharing God's Word

Read together John 16:5–7. Emphasize that the disciples listened to Jesus and trusted that his promise that the Advocate, the Holy Spirit, would come to them would come true.

Praying

In this chapter your child prayed part of the Prayer to the Holy Spirit that is prayed by the Church on Pentecost. Read and pray together this prayer on page 75.

Making a Difference

Choose one of the following activities to do as a family or design a similar activity of your own.

- Pray the Prayer to the Holy Spirit on page 75 as your family prayer this week. Remember that the Holy Spirit is always with you as your advocate and teacher.

- When you take part in Mass this week, find the ambry. The ambry is a special place where the sacred oils that are used in the celebration of the liturgy are kept. Recall that all the baptized are anointed with the sacred oil of chrism at Confirmation as the words "Be sealed with the Gift of the Holy Spirit" are prayed.

- Read together John 16:5–7. Talk about how the Holy Spirit helps your family.

For more ideas on ways your family can live your faith, visit the "Faith First for Families" page at **www.FaithFirst.com**. The "Make a Difference" page goes especially well with this chapter.

Different Gifts, the Same Spirit

9

We Pray

When you send forth
your breath, they
are created,
and you renew the
face of the earth.
PSALM 104:30

Come, Holy Spirit,
fill our hearts
with light
and lead us
to all truth.   Amen.

*What does it mean to say
that a person or group has
"spirit"?*

Having spirit is an
important quality of a
person. God has given the
Church the gift of the
Holy Spirit.

*What does it mean to the
Church to have the gift of
the Holy Spirit?*

The Work of the Holy Spirit

Faith Vocabulary

charisms. Graces, or gifts, given by the Holy Spirit to build up the Church on earth for the good of all people and the needs of the world.

Sacred Tradition. The passing on of the teachings of Christ by the Church through the power and guidance of the Holy Spirit.

Images of the Holy Spirit

Christians are people of the Holy Spirit. The Holy Spirit lives within the whole Church and within each member of the Church. The Church uses many images to help us understand the presence and work of the Holy Spirit. Here are two of those images.

A Mighty Wind. When Jesus promised that the holy "Spirit" would come to them, the disciples were not hearing a new word. They heard about the work of a "mighty wind" (Genesis 1:2), a *ruah*—the Hebrew word for "spirit" in the story of creation.

The Breath of God. This "mighty wind" is also the "breath," or "spirit," of God the disciples prayed about in the Psalms:

When you send forth your
   breath, they are
   created,
and you renew the face
   of the earth.
   PSALM 104:30

The Spirit Promised by the Prophets

Later in the history of the Israelites, the prophets often spoke of God's promise to send a new spirit upon all people. Ezekiel wrote:

"I will give you a new heart and place a new spirit within you, taking from your bodies your stony hearts and giving you natural hearts."
   EZEKIEL 36:26

The Church has come to understand that the Spirit in the Old Testament is the Holy Spirit, the third Person of the Holy Trinity.

Give an example of a "stony heart," for example, lying to avoid being embarrassed. Then describe the "new heart" that replaces it, for example, telling the truth.

Descent of Holy Spirit upon Mary and the Apostles at Pentecost, stained glass

The Holy Spirit in the Church

At the very beginning of his public ministry, Jesus said:

"The Spirit of the Lord is upon me." LUKE 4:18

The Gospels tell us that the Holy Spirit was at work in the life of Jesus from the announcement of his birth to his Ascension and promise that the Holy Spirit would come to the disciples.

After receiving the Holy Spirit on Pentecost, Peter courageously and clearly preached about Jesus. Moved by the Holy Spirit, over three thousand people asked to be baptized that day.

The Church is the Temple of the Holy Spirit. The Holy Spirit blesses each of us with **charisms**, or special graces that we are to use to help build up the Church. Saint Paul wrote:

There are different kinds of spiritual gifts but the same Spirit; there are different forms of service but the same Lord; there are different workings but the same God who produces all of them in everyone.

1 CORINTHIANS 12:4–6

Describe one way you can work with the Holy Spirit to build up the Church on earth.

bishops teach clearly and authentically what God has revealed through Scripture and **Sacred Tradition.** Sacred Tradition is the passing on of the teachings of Christ by the Church through the power and guidance of the Holy Spirit.

Our Sanctifier. The Holy Spirit is the One who makes us holy. Through the Holy Spirit, we receive sanctifying grace. This is the gift of holiness that makes us sharers in the very life and love of God. We also receive actual graces. This is the help the Holy Spirit gives us to live as Jesus taught.

The Holy Spirit makes us one with Christ and each other. The Holy Spirit is and will continue to be at work helping the Church prepare for the coming of the kingdom of God. At that time Christ will come again in glory and his work on earth will be finished.

Create a saying for this banner that shows the Holy Spirit is active in the world today.

The Holy Spirit Today

The Holy Spirit is active in the Church today. The Holy Spirit is our teacher and sanctifier.

Our Teacher. The Holy Spirit guides us in understanding and teaching what God has revealed in Jesus Christ. The Holy Spirit helps the pope and the

Our Church Makes a Difference

Katharine Drexel near Lukachukai, Arizona, in 1927, where she established a day school

Our Catholic Identity

Fruits of the Holy Spirit

In Galatians 5:22–23 Saint Paul lists the signs that show that the Holy Spirit is alive in the Church. They are called the fruits of the Holy Spirit. They are love, joy, peace, patience, kindness, generosity, faithfulness, gentleness, and self-control. The tradition of the Church also includes goodness, modesty, and chastity as fruits of the Holy Spirit.

Saint Katharine Drexel

The Holy Spirit is always at work in the world. He is the same Spirit who was at work in the life of Jesus during his work on earth. From the time of the Apostles, the Holy Spirit has helped the Church continue the work, or mission, Jesus gave to his disciples.

Some Christians leave their homes and families and travel great distances to preach and live the Gospel. Many leave their own country and work with people living in other lands. We call these people missionaries.

Katharine Drexel was a missionary who lived and worked in the United States. She left her home and family to live the Gospel. She used her family inheritance to work with Native Americans and African Americans in the United States. Today, members of the religious community founded by Saint Katharine Drexel continue the missionary work she began.

We do not have to travel very far to do what Jesus asks us. How can you be a missionary?

What Difference Does Faith Make in My Life?

The Holy Spirit gives you gifts, or charisms, to continue the work of Jesus wherever you are.

A magazine has decided to write an article about you. They have learned what you are doing to make your neighborhood a better place. Write the opening paragraph of the article. Include the role the Holy Spirit has in your helping others.

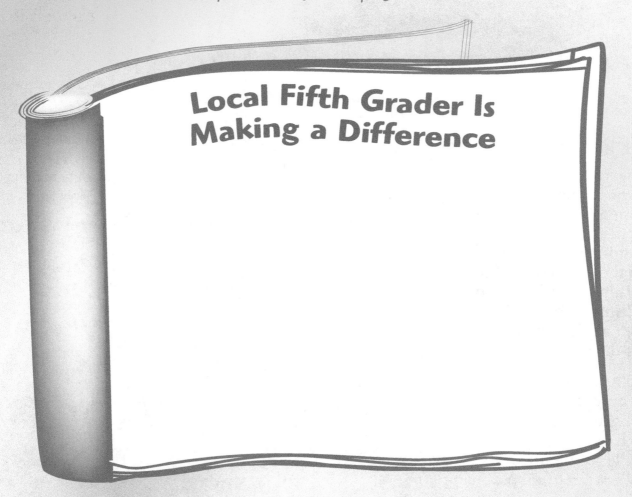

Local Fifth Grader Is Making a Difference

My Faith Choice

This week I will use one of the gifts the Holy Spirit has given me to make the world a better place. I will use the gift of

_____

to _____.

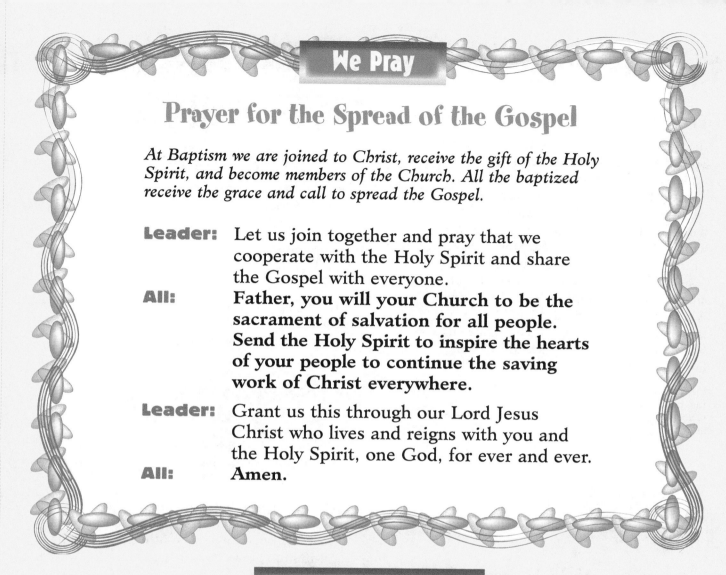

Prayer for the Spread of the Gospel

At Baptism we are joined to Christ, receive the gift of the Holy Spirit, and become members of the Church. All the baptized receive the grace and call to spread the Gospel.

Leader: Let us join together and pray that we cooperate with the Holy Spirit and share the Gospel with everyone.

All: **Father, you will your Church to be the sacrament of salvation for all people. Send the Holy Spirit to inspire the hearts of your people to continue the saving work of Christ everywhere.**

Leader: Grant us this through our Lord Jesus Christ who lives and reigns with you and the Holy Spirit, one God, for ever and ever.

All: **Amen.**

We Remember

Use words from this chapter to complete the sentences.

1. __mighty wind__ and __bless of God__ are two images for the Holy Spirit.

2. The Holy Spirit blesses us with __carcisoms__ to continue the work of Christ.

3. The Holy Spirit dwells in the __world__ today.

4. The Holy Spirit is the _____, or the One who makes us holy.

5. The Holy Spirit helps the _____ and the _____ to authentically teach what Jesus taught.

To Help You Remember

1. The Holy Spirit helps the Church teach about Jesus as Saint Peter and the other Apostles did.

2. The Holy Spirit guides the Church to pass on the teachings of Christ.

3. The Holy Spirit sanctifies the Church, or makes the Church holy.

This Week . . .

In chapter 9, "Different Gifts, the Same Spirit," your child deepened their understanding of and faith in the Holy Spirit. They learned that the images of wind and breath help us understand the work of the Holy Spirit in the Church, which is the Temple of the Holy Spirit. The Holy Spirit was active in the life of Jesus and has been active in the Church since its very beginning. The Holy Spirit is our teacher and guide. The Holy Spirit is our sanctifier, the One who makes us holy and gives us the grace to live holy lives.

For more on the teachings of the Catholic Church on the mystery of the Holy Spirit, see *Catechism of the Catholic Church* paragraph numbers 691–693, 797–801, and 1091–1109.

Sharing God's Word

Read together 1 Corinthians 12:4–7. Emphasize that the Holy Spirit gives each of the baptized special graces, or charisms, to help them continue the work of Christ.

Praying

In this chapter your child prayed a prayer for the spread of the Gospel. Read and pray together this prayer on page 83.

Making a Difference

Choose one of the following activities to do as a family or design a similar activity of your own.

- Take turns telling one another what special talents, or gifts, you see in each other. Encourage each other to use their gifts to spread the Gospel.

- Talk about how the Holy Spirit can help us make good decisions and choices. Choose to do one thing this week to help others.

- Find out more about Saint Katharine Drexel or another saint. Talk about how this saint used their gifts to continue the work of Jesus Christ. Look for information about saints at your parish library or visit the *Catholic Encyclopedia* Web site on the Internet.

For more ideas on ways your family can live your faith, visit the "Faith First for Families" page at **www.FaithFirst.com**. Click on "Games" and make learning fun for your child.

Thy Kingdom Come!

10

We Pray

Happy are those who
  dwell in your house!
They never cease to
  praise you.   PSALM 84:5

Our Father,
who art in heaven.
Thy kingdom come.
                    Amen.

*Why is it so much easier to
do a project when people
work together?*

We all like to work with
other people. The Church
is the People of God. We
work together to continue
the work of Jesus Christ
until the end of time.

*How would you describe the
work that the Church does?*

Faith Focus

What words and images describe the work of the Church?

Faith Vocabulary

Church. The Body of Christ; the new People of God called together in Christ by the power of the Holy Spirit.

kingdom of God. All people and creation living in communion with God at the end of time when the work of Christ will be completed and he will come again in glory.

The Body of Christ

The Holy Spirit has invited us to belong to the community of the **Church.** Saint Paul the Apostle used the image of a human body to help us understand what it means to belong to the Church. He wrote:

> As a body is one though it has many parts, and all the parts of the body, though many, are one body, so also Christ. For in one Spirit we were all baptized into one body.
>
> 1 CORINTHIANS 12:12–13

Christ is the Head of his Body, the Church. All the faithful are its members. Each of us has a different role or responsibility in the Church.

Laity, or Lay Faithful. Almost all of the baptized are members of the laity. We all have the responsibility to work together to serve the world as Jesus did.

Ordained Ministers. The Holy Spirit calls some members of the Body of Christ to serve the whole Church as bishops, priests, and deacons. They form the clergy. The pope is the bishop of Rome. He is the pastor of the Church on earth.

Religious Communities. Some of the laity and ordained consecrate their lives to God in a special way and live as members of religious communities. They support one another in living their Baptism and serve the Church in many ways.

The Marks of the Church

The Church, the Body of Christ, has four essential characteristics that identify her as the Church founded by Jesus. These characteristics are called the Marks of the Church.

The Church is one. We believe in one faith and one Lord, and we share one Baptism.

The Church is holy. Our sharing in the life of the Holy Trinity is the source of the Church's holiness.

The Church is catholic. The Church reaches out to all people and welcomes them into the family of God's Church.

The Church is apostolic. We trace our faith back to the Apostles. The pope and other bishops are the successors of the Apostles. They share in the responsibility Jesus gave to the Apostles to teach in his name and make all people disciples of Jesus.

True members of the Church share the faith of the Church and believe what the Church teaches. They pray together and celebrate the sacraments together with Christ and the Holy Spirit. They serve others by sharing Jesus' healing, forgiveness, and hope with all people.

Design a bookmark that describes one of the Marks of the Church.

Eternal Life

The Church continues the work of Christ and prepares the way for the coming of the **kingdom of God.** Jesus taught that the kingdom of God was a place of eternal happiness. It would fully come about at the end of time, and there will be "new heavens and a new earth" (2 Peter 3:13).

At the moment of death our lives will be individually judged by God. Life after death includes heaven, purgatory, and hell.

Heaven. All those who have been faithful to God will live with God the Father, Jesus, and the Holy Spirit in happiness forever.

Purgatory. Some people are not ready to receive the gift of eternal happiness at the moment of their death. God will give them the opportunity to grow in their love for him to prepare them for heaven. This opportunity is called purgatory.

Hell. When people sin seriously and do not ask God for forgiveness, they choose to stay separated from God now and forever. We call this separation from God hell.

At the end of time at the Last Judgment, all who have been faithful to God will be called forth to live in heaven. All the faithful believers in Christ form the Communion of Saints. The Communion of Saints includes all those who are faithful to God—those in heaven, those in purgatory, and those living on earth.

Write or draw an example of one way we can help prepare the way for the coming of the kingdom of God.

Thy Kingdom Come!

Our Church Makes a Difference

Devotion to Mary

Christians have always honored the saints. We honor Mary, the mother of Jesus, above all the other saints. God has brought Mary, with her body and soul, to heaven, where she lives in the glory of her Son. We call this the Assumption of Mary.

Mary, whom we honor as Queen of Heaven, reminds us that at the end of time we too shall live forever with a new body, a resurrected body. The original plan of God for us to live in happiness with him will be restored.

Catholics in the United States honor Mary as the Patroness of the United States of America. We honor her under the title of the Immaculate Conception. This professes our faith that Mary was free from original and all personal sin from the very first moment of her conception and that she remained free from all sin throughout her entire life.

Other countries in the Americas also honor Mary, using other titles. In Puerto Rico Mary is honored as Our Lady of Providence; in Costa Rica, as Our Lady of the Angels; in the Dominican Republic, as Our Lady of Altagracia; and in Cuba, as Our Lady of Caridad del Cobre. Mary, Our Lady of Guadalupe, is the patroness of all the Americas.

How do you and your family honor Mary? How do you show your love for her?

Our Catholic Identity

The Rosary

One way that Catholics deepen their love for Jesus and Mary is by praying the Rosary. Praying the mysteries of the Rosary puts us in touch with the heart of our faith. The mysteries of the Rosary are the events in the life of Jesus and Mary that we consider and pray over.

The Basilica of the National Shrine of the Immaculate Conception, Washington, D.C. The patronal church of the United States.

What Difference Does Faith Make in My Life?

You are a member of the Church, the Body of Christ. The Holy Spirit helps you use your gifts, as Mary and the saints did, to prepare for the coming of the kingdom of God.

Think about your talents, or gifts. Then list three of your gifts. Describe how you can use those gifts to work together with other members of the Church to prepare the way for the coming of the kingdom of God.

Thy Kingdom Come

Gifts _____

_____ .

How I can use them _____

_____

_____

_____

_____

_____

_____

_____ .

My Faith Choice

This week I will try to use my gifts to continue the work of Christ. I will

_____

_____ .

Thy Kingdom Come

The Our Father, or Lord's Prayer, is a summary of the Gospel. Join hands and pray the Our Father.

Group 1: Our Father, who art in heaven,
Group 2: hallowed be thy name;

Group 1: thy kingdom come;
Group 2: thy will be done on earth as it is in heaven.

Group 1: Give us this day our daily bread;
Group 2: and forgive us our trespasses
as we forgive those who trespass against us;

Group 1: and lead us not into temptation,
Group 2: but deliver us from evil.

All: **Amen.**

We Remember

Name the four Marks of the Church. Design four symbols to describe the four Marks of the Church.

To Help You Remember

1. The Church, the Body of Christ, is made up of the lay faithful, the ordained, and members of religious communities.

2. The Church that Jesus founded has four essential characteristics, or marks. They are one, holy, catholic, and apostolic.

3. All the members of the Church work together to prepare for the coming of the kingdom of God.

This Week . . .

In chapter 10, "Thy Kingdom Come!" your child learned that all the members of the Church, the one Body of Christ, have different roles and responsibilities to continue the work of Christ. The Holy Spirit is guiding the Church to continue that work until the end of time. At the end of time, there will be "new heavens and a new earth." The kingdom of God will be established in its fullness, and God's original plan of happiness will be restored in Christ.

For more on the teachings of the Catholic Church on the mystery of the Church, the Communion of Saints, and the life everlasting, see *Catechism of the Catholic Church* paragraph numbers 668–679, 787–795, and 811–972.

Sharing God's Word

Read together Saint Paul's teaching on the Church as the Body of Christ in 1 Corinthians 12:12–31. Emphasize that Christ is the Head of his Body, the Church. All of the baptized are its members.

Praying

In this chapter your child prayed the Our Father. Pray the Our Father as a family.

Making a Difference

Choose one of the following activities to do as a family or design a similar activity of your own.

- Pray the Our Father at mealtimes this week. Praise God and ask him for grace to strengthen you to prepare the way for the coming of the kingdom.

- Talk about all the ways your parish continues the work of Christ. If you need ideas, look in the parish bulletin. Decide one way you can work as a family with other members of your parish to continue the work of Christ.

- The Church reaches out to all people. Do something this week to reach out to others.

For more ideas on ways your family can live your faith, visit the "Faith First for Families" page at **www.FaithFirst.com**. Click on "Make a Difference" to discover how your family can continue the work of Christ.

Unit 1 Review

A. Best Response

Read each statement and circle the best answer.

1. In whom does God reveal himself most fully?
   a. the prophets
   b. the baptized
   c. Jesus Christ
   d. the Church

2. Where in the Bible do you read about the life, death, and Resurrection of Jesus?
   a. Psalms
   b. Gospels
   c. Proverbs
   d. Torah

3. What is the central belief of the Christian faith?
   a. Annunciation
   b. Our Father
   c. Holy Trinity
   d. Ascension

4. Which one of the following is not an attribute of God?
   a. holy
   b. powerless
   c. truth
   d. almighty

5. What mystery of faith tells us Jesus is true God and true man?
   a. Annunciation
   b. Creation
   c. Holy Trinity
   d. Incarnation

6. What are the most important events of Jesus' life?
   a. the Paschal Mystery
   b. the Last Supper
   c. the Annunciation
   d. Pentecost

7. Which of the following is not an image of the Holy Spirit?
   a. a rainbow
   b. the breath of God
   c. a mighty wind
   d. a dove

8. Who are not ordained ministers of the Church?
   a. bishops
   b. deacons
   c. priests
   d. lectors

9. What are the four Marks of the Church?
   a. one, holy, joyful, catholic
   b. holy, faithful, catholic, apostolic
   c. one, holy, catholic, apostolic
   d. one, holy, diverse, catholic

10. What is Mary's relationship to the Church?
    a. Mother of God
    b. Mother of the Church
    c. Mother of Jesus
    d. all of the above

B. Matching Words and Phrases

1. *Use the terms in the word bank to finish these sentences from the Nicene Creed.*

> **Father**   **Son**   **Holy Spirit**   **Lord**   **creator**

   a. I believe in one God, the _____ almighty, maker of heaven and earth, of all things visible and invisible.

   b. I believe in one _____ Jesus Christ, the only _____ of God.

   c. I believe in the _____, the Lord, the giver of life.

2. *Match the faith terms in column A with their descriptions in column B.*

Column A

_____ 1. miracle

_____ 2. Evangelists

_____ 3. Sacred Tradition

_____ 4. Church

_____ 5. charisms

Column B

a. teachings of Christ passed on by the Church

b. graces given by the Holy Spirit to build up the Church on earth

c. the new People of God, or the Body of Christ

d. an action that goes beyond the laws of nature

e. the writers of the four Gospels

C. What I Have Learned

1. *Write three things you learned in this unit. Share them with the group.*

_____

_____

_____

2. *Look at the list of faith terms in "Words to Know" on page 12. Circle the terms you know now.*

D. From a Scripture Story

The story of Jesus calming the storm at sea invites us to believe and trust in him. Write two more ideas that you learned from this Gospel story.

_____

_____

What works of the Church do these pictures show?

95

Getting Ready

What I Have Learned

What is something you already know about these three faith terms?

The Eucharist

_____

_____

The Sacraments of Healing

_____

_____

The Christian vocation

_____

_____

Words to Know

Put an X next to the faith terms you know. Put a ? next to the faith terms you need to know more about.

Faith Vocabulary

_____ liturgy

_____ Baptism

_____ Confirmation

_____ Pentecost

_____ Eucharist

_____ sacrifice

_____ breaking of bread

_____ epistle

_____ Reconciliation

_____ Anointing of the Sick

Questions I Have

What questions would you like to ask about the Eucharist?

_____

_____

_____

_____

A Scripture Story

Christians reading a letter
from Saint Paul the Apostle

Why did Saint Paul write letters to the Christians to whom he had preached the Gospel?

Celebrating the Liturgy

We Pray

We thank you, God,
  we give thanks;
 we call upon your name,
  declare your
    wonderful deeds.

PSALM 75:2

Father,
all-powerful and
ever-living God, we
give you thanks always
and everywhere
through Jesus Christ,
our Lord.   Amen.

*How do you show your
thanks to people?*

Gracias. Asante. Cám ón.
All these words mean
"thank you." The Church,
the People of God, gathers
at Mass to thank God.

*What are some of the ways
you thank God at Mass?*

We Worship God

Faith Focus

Why do we celebrate the liturgy and sacraments as a community?

Faith Vocabulary

liturgy. The work of the Church, the People of God, of worshiping him through which Christ continues the work of Redemption in, with, and through his Church.

sacraments. The seven main liturgical signs of the Church, given to the Church by Jesus Christ, that make his saving work present and make us sharers in the life of God, the Holy Trinity.

The Liturgy

The work of the People of God, the Church, is the worship of God. We gather to pray, honor, thank, and give glory to God for all he has done and continues to do for us.

When the Church comes together to worship God, we celebrate **liturgy**. The word *liturgy* means "work of the people." The liturgy of the Church includes the celebration of the seven **sacraments** and the Liturgy of the Hours.

The Holy Trinity is present with the Church when we come together to celebrate the liturgy. We worship one God in three Persons, the Holy Trinity. We pray to the Father, through the Son, and in the Holy Spirit.

Each time we celebrate the liturgy, we share more fully in the new life Jesus gained for us.

- We are changed.
- We become more like Jesus.
- We find strength to live as Jesus wants us to live.
- We bring Jesus' life and love to the world.

When the Church celebrates the liturgy, we join with Jesus Christ, and through the power of the Holy Spirit we remember and share in the Paschal Mystery. We are made sharers in his Passion, death, Resurrection, and Ascension.

Illustrate with words or pictures one way you try to bring Jesus' life and love to the world.

The Liturgical Year

The Church celebrates the liturgy every day and all year long. This yearly cycle of the Church's celebration of the liturgy is called the liturgical year. All year long, each and every day, we hear and take part in God's great plan of saving love for us.

The liturgical year is a "year of the Lord's grace." It is the celebration of the mysteries of the birth, life, death, Resurrection, and Ascension of Jesus. It includes weekly celebrations of Sunday, the Lord's Day, the yearly cycle of the seasons of the Church's year, and feasts of the Lord and of Mary and the other saints.

The Year of the Lord's Grace

Advent. During Advent the Church celebrates God's coming among us. We get ready to remember Jesus' birth on Christmas Day. We remember Jesus' promise to come again in glory at the end of time.

Christmas. We remember and celebrate that the Son of God, Jesus the Savior, came and lived among us.

Lent. With the help of the Holy Spirit we strive to grow in our life in Christ. We support those preparing to be baptized at Easter. We prepare to renew our own baptismal promises.

Triduum. This three-day celebration of Holy Thursday, Good Friday, and Easter Vigil/Easter Sunday is the heart and center of the liturgical year.

Easter. For fifty days we joyfully reflect on the Resurrection and our new life in Christ. On the fiftieth day of the celebration, we celebrate the feast of Pentecost.

Ordinary Time. The other weeks of the year are called Ordinary Time. We listen to what Jesus said and did and learn ways to live our life as his followers.

Describe some of the ways you see your parish celebrating the seasons of the liturgical year.

The Seven Sacraments

Before Jesus returned to his Father, he promised that he would always be with us. Jesus is especially present with his Church when we celebrate the sacraments. Jesus gave us the sacraments. The sacraments are the seven main celebrations of the liturgy. They are signs of God's work among us. They put us in contact with the saving work of Jesus Christ. He touches our lives through the sacraments, and we are changed.

Sacraments of Christian Initiation. Baptism, Confirmation, and Eucharist are called Sacraments of Christian Initiation. Through these three sacraments we are joined to Christ and become full members of the Church. We are made sharers in God's life and receive help to live as children of God.

Sacraments of Healing. Penance and Reconciliation and Anointing of the Sick are the Sacraments of Healing. Through these sacraments we celebrate and share in God's healing love.

Sacraments at the Service of Communion. Holy Orders and Matrimony are the Sacraments at the Service of Communion. Through these sacraments some members of the Church are consecrated to serve the whole Body of Christ, the Church. The word *consecrated* means "set aside for a holy purpose."

All the sacraments build up the Body of Christ. They make us sharers in God's life and love and give us the help to live as children of God. We are changed more completely into the image of Christ. Our life with the Holy Trinity is strengthened.

For each of the letters in the word SACRAMENT, write a word that says something about the sacraments. Use each word to share what happens when the Church celebrates the sacraments.

S \
A \
C \
R \
A \
M \
E \
N \
T

The Holy Bible

Our Church Makes a Difference

Feasts of the Lord

The Church proclaims the wonderful works of God among us when we celebrate the liturgy. In addition to the cycle of the seasons of the Church's year and the feasts of the Lord connected with those seasons, the Church celebrates other feasts of the Lord. The feast of the Sacred Heart of Jesus and the feast of the Triumph of the Cross are two of those feasts.

The Sacred Heart of Jesus and the cross are both symbols of the love of Jesus. Jesus commanded that his followers are to love and serve one another as he serves and loves us. The celebration of the liturgy is always a proclamation to the world of the saving work of Christ and a call to a life of service. Celebrating these feasts deepens our faith in the mystery of Christ's sacrificial love for us. It strengthens us to live out that love in our service of God and others.

How do you see the people of your parish living as signs of God's love?

Sacred Heart of Jesus, stained glass

What Difference Does Faith Make in My Life?

You join with Christ and other members of the Church throughout the year to celebrate the liturgy. Each season of the Church's liturgical year helps you grow and live your faith.

Choose a liturgical season. Create and design this banner to help you celebrate it. Include a message about living the season. Be sure to use the liturgical color for that season.

Celebrating Our Faith

My Faith Choice

This week I will worship God in all I do and say. I will

_____

_____.

Lift Up Your Heart

The liturgy is the Church's work of worshiping God. Learn to pray this simple prayer of praise and honor to God that we pray at Mass. Pray it over and over again quietly in your heart.

Leader: Let us lift up our hearts and give thanks and praise to God.

Group 1: Holy, Holy, Holy Lord God of hosts.

Group 2: Heaven and earth are full of your glory.

All: **Hosanna in the highest.**

Group 1: Blessed is he who comes in the name of the Lord.

Group 2: Blessed is he who comes in the name of the Lord.

All: **Hosanna in the highest.**

BASED ON PREFACE ACCLAMATION

We Remember

Match the faith terms in the left column with the descriptions in the right column.

Terms

___ 1. sacraments

___ 2. Paschal Mystery

___ 3. Lent

___ 4. Easter

___ 5. Sacraments of Christian Initiation

___ 6. liturgy

Descriptions

a. Jesus' Passion, death, Resurrection, and glorious Ascension

b. a season of the Church's year that prepares us for Easter

c. sacraments by which we are joined to Christ and become members of the Church

d. work of the People of God

e. seven liturgical celebrations of the Church given to us by Christ

f. a season of the Church during which we rejoice in Christ's Resurrection

To Help You Remember

1. The liturgy is the Church's work of worshiping God.

2. The liturgical year is the Church's cycle of worship that celebrates God's great plan of saving love for us.

3. The sacraments make the saving work of Jesus Christ present to us and make us sharers in the life of God, the Holy Trinity.

This Week . . .

In chapter 11, "Celebrating the Liturgy," your child learned about the liturgy, the Church's work of worshiping God. The liturgy includes the celebration of the sacraments. Sacraments are the signs of God's work among us that Jesus gave us. Jesus touches our lives through the sacraments, and we are changed. Like the calendar year, the Church's liturgical year of worship is made up of a cycle of seasons and feast days. The Easter Triduum, or three days, of Holy Thursday, Good Friday, and the Easter Vigil/Easter Sunday is the heart of the liturgical year. The seasons of the Church's year are Advent, Christmas, Lent, Easter, and Ordinary Time.

For more on the teachings of the Catholic Church on the liturgy and the sacraments in general, see *Catechism of the Catholic Church* paragraph numbers 1135–1186.

Sharing God's Word

Read together Psalm 75:2. Emphasize that our whole life should give honor and glory and praise to God.

Praying

In this chapter your child learned a prayer of praise and honor to God. Read and pray together this prayer on page 103.

Making a Difference

Choose one of the following activities to do as a family or design a similar activity of your own.

- Invite each family member to share which of the liturgical seasons they like best. Talk about how this season helps them give praise and thanks to God.

- Decorate your home according to the current liturgical season. Allow the decorations to help you remember that God is always with you.

- When your family takes part in the celebration of Mass this week, pay close attention to the liturgical colors and decorations. Talk about how the liturgical season helps you remember and share in God's great plan of saving love for the world.

For more ideas on ways your family can live your faith, visit the "Faith First for Families" page at **www.FaithFirst.com**. Click on "Games" to review the seven sacraments with your child.

Baptism and Confirmation

12

We Pray

O God our savior, . . .
You visit the earth and
 water it,
 make it abundantly
 fertile.   PSALM 65:6, 10

**Father, in Baptism
we use your gift of
water and you give us
the grace of new life
in Christ.   Amen.**

*What would your life be
like without water?*

Water is essential for life.
Imagine a day without
water. The Church uses
water to celebrate Baptism,
the sacrament of new life
in Christ.

*Why is water the best symbol
for Baptism?*

Faith Focus

What are the effects of Baptism and Confirmation?

Faith Vocabulary

Baptism. The Sacrament of Christian Initiation in which we are first joined to Jesus Christ, become members of the Church, are reborn as God's adopted children, receive the gift of the Holy Spirit, and original sin and personal sins are forgiven.

Confirmation. The Sacrament of Christian Initiation that strengthens the graces of Baptism and in which our new life in Christ is sealed by the gift of the Holy Spirit.

Celebrating Baptism

Baptism is one of the three Sacraments of Christian Initiation. It is the first sacrament we receive.

Here is a summary of the rite of Baptism. Each part shows that the people being baptized are receiving the gift of new life from God.

The Rite of Baptism

Blessing of the water. After the celebration of the Liturgy of the Word, the priest or deacon greets everyone at the baptismal font or baptismal pool. He says, "My dear brothers and sisters, God uses the sacrament of water to give his divine life to those who believe in him." Blessing the water, he retells the story of salvation.

Renunciation of sin and profession of faith. All present join with those to be baptized and reject sin. All promise to live as God's children. All profess faith in God, the Holy Trinity.

Baptism in water. The person to be baptized now enters, or is immersed in, the water or has water poured on his or her head three times, as the celebrant says the words, "(Name), I baptize you in the name of the Father, and of the Son, and of the Holy Spirit."

Anointing with chrism. The celebrant anoints the top of the head of each of the newly baptized with the holy oil of chrism. This shows that the Holy Spirit is with the baptized to strengthen them to live as members of the Body of Christ, the Church.

White garment and lighted candle. The newly baptized receive a white garment and a candle lighted from the Easter candle. Clothed in Christ, the baptized are to keep the flame of faith alive in their hearts.

Effects of Baptism

All the parts of the rite of Baptism point to the deeper meaning of what we are seeing and hearing. We call what happens at Baptism the effects of Baptism.

Children of the Father. In the Gospel story about Nicodemus, Jesus tells Nicodemus that he needs to be reborn of water and the Holy Spirit (see John 3:5). Through Baptism we receive new life in Jesus Christ as children of God the Father. We are born again.

Members of the Church, the Body of Christ. We are joined to Christ through Baptism. We become members of the Body of Christ, the Church. We become part of a larger family of faith, the Church.

Temples of the Holy Spirit. The New Testament tells us that we are temples of the Holy Spirit. Through Baptism we receive the gift of the Holy Spirit. Living as a member of the Body of Christ is not something we do alone. The Holy Spirit lives within us. Throughout our lives the Holy Spirit invites and helps us live as children of God and followers of Jesus Christ.

Forgiveness of sin. Baptism frees us from original sin and all the personal sins that we may have committed. Everything that separates us from God is washed away. We receive the gift of sanctifying grace. We are made sharers in the life of God, the Holy Trinity.

In this candle, describe one thing you might do to live your Baptism.

Celebrating Confirmation

Confirmation seals, or completes, our Baptism. It is the second Sacrament of Christian Initiation. The bishop is the usual minister of this sacrament, but sometimes the bishop names a priest to celebrate Confirmation. This usually happens when people are confirmed at the Easter Vigil in their parish church.

Each part of the rite of Confirmation shows how the Holy Spirit strengthens our Baptism. One of the images that the Bible uses to teach us about the Holy Spirit is fire. Filled with the Holy Spirit, our hearts are "on fire" to live our Baptism. Sealed with the gift of the Holy Spirit, we are strengthened to continue the work of Christ.

The Rite of Confirmation

Laying on of hands. The bishop holds out his hands and extends them over the candidates for Confirmation. He prays, asking God, the Father of our Lord Jesus Christ, to pour out the Holy Spirit upon them to be their Helper and Guide.

Anointing with chrism. One by one the candidates with their sponsors go to the bishop. The sponsor places his or her right hand on the shoulder of the candidate and presents the candidate by name to the bishop. The bishop places his right hand on top of the head of the candidate and makes a sign of the cross on the candidate's forehead with chrism. As he does this, he prays, "(Name), be sealed with the Gift of the Holy Spirit." Anointing is a sign that God is calling the confirmed and giving them the grace to serve his people.

The newly confirmed says he or she believes what is happening by responding, "Amen." The bishop then says, "Peace be with you." The newly confirmed responds, "And with your spirit."

Describe what you can do at home, in school, or in your neighborhood that continues the work of Jesus Christ. Share your ideas with the class.

_____

_____

_____

_____

_____

Our Church Makes a Difference

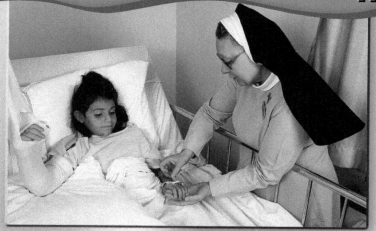

Lights of Faith

Some Christians are called to live their Baptism and Confirmation as members of a religious order or religious congregation. These communities are groups of either men or women who consecrate their lives to the service of the Gospel of Jesus Christ. They are lights of faith in the world.

Religious communities commit themselves to prayer and the Corporal and Spiritual Works of Mercy. They strive to live the gifts of the Holy Spirit. Some religious communities, such as the Trappists and Poor Clares, devote themselves to a life of prayer. Other communities, such as the Dominicans and Jesuits, combine their life of prayer with a life of serving others. Other religious communities serve people who are poor, sick, or homeless.

Some work with people in prisons and with those suffering from injustice. Others help with the Church's work of education. Other religious communities serve God and people as missionaries.

All religious communities keep the flame of faith burning brightly in the world. They work to bring about a world according to the plan of God in which all people live in peace and justice.

How do members of religious communities live their Baptism? How does this bring about God's plan for a world of peace and justice?

What Difference Does Faith Make in My Life?

The Holy Spirit lives within you and gives you the grace to live the Gospel and be a light in the world.

Illustrate a scene that shows what fifth graders might do to live the Gospel.

My Faith Choice

This week I will try to live my Baptism. I will

_____

_____.

Prayer for the Gifts of the Holy Spirit

The Holy Spirit lives within the Church and within each member of the Church. The Holy Spirit is always strengthening us to live the Gospel. Pray this prayer together.

Leader: God, Father of our Lord Jesus Christ,
send us the gifts of the Holy Spirit.
Send us the spirit of wisdom and understanding.

All: **May your Holy Spirit continue to work
in the world through all who believe.**

Leader: Send us the spirit of right judgment and counsel.

All: **May your Holy Spirit continue to work
in the world through all who believe.**

Leader: Send us the spirit of knowledge and reverence.

All: **May your Holy Spirit continue to work
in the world through all who believe.**

Leader: Send us the spirit of wonder and awe.

All: **May your Holy Spirit continue to work
in the world through all who believe.**

We Remember

Circle the sacrament words hidden in the puzzle. Describe what each word tells about becoming a follower of Jesus Christ.

```
E R T Y Y A N O I N T I N G H K E

W M Q F B B A P T I S M Q E R V I

X N C O N F I R M A T I O N Q L S

N H J O P S K A W A T E R D F S Z
```

To Help You Remember

1. Baptism, Confirmation, and Eucharist are the three Sacraments of Christian Initiation.

2. In Baptism we are joined to Christ, and original sin and our personal sins are forgiven. We are reborn as God's children. We receive the gift of the Holy Spirit and become members of the Church.

3. In Confirmation we are sealed with the gift of the Holy Spirit, and the graces of Baptism are strengthened.

This Week . . .

In chapter 12, "Baptism and Confirmation," your child learned more about the celebration and effects of Baptism and Confirmation. Baptism brings us into new life in Christ and makes us members of the Body of Christ, the Church. Through Baptism we receive the gift of the Holy Spirit. By God's gift, through water and the Holy Spirit, original sin and everything that separates us from God is washed away. Confirmation confirms, or seals, our Baptism. The Holy Spirit strengthens us with his sevenfold gifts to live the Gospel and proclaim Jesus Christ to others.

For more on the teachings of the Catholic Church on the sacraments of Baptism and Confirmation, see *Catechism of the Catholic Church* paragraph numbers 1210–1274 and 1285–1314.

Sharing God's Word

Read together Luke 4:16–22. Emphasize that through Baptism we receive the gift of the Holy Spirit and in Confirmation we are sealed with the gift of the Holy Spirit.

Praying

In this chapter your child prayed for the gifts of the Holy Spirit. Read and pray together this prayer on page 111.

Making a Difference

Choose one of the following activities to do as a family or design a similar activity of your own.

- When your family participates in Mass this week, go to the ambry after Mass. The ambry is the place where the chrism and other sacred oils used in the celebration of the liturgy are kept. Recall that we are anointed with chrism at Baptism and Confirmation.

- Look at your family photo albums and find Baptism pictures. Share stories about each person's Baptism. Talk about who was there and why Baptism is an important family day.

- Talk about all the ways your family lives Baptism.

For more ideas on ways your family can live your faith, visit the "Faith First for Families" page at **www.FaithFirst.com**. Click on "Contemporary Issues" this week to find an article on an especially interesting topic.

Pentecost
A Scripture Story

13

We Pray

Give thanks to the LORD,
  invoke his name;
  make known among
  the peoples his
  deeds!   PSALM 105:1

God our Father,
may the work of the
Holy Spirit continue
through all who
believe in Jesus Christ,
your only Son.   Amen.

*Why is it important for
countries or groups to
celebrate their beginnings?*

On the Fourth of July you
can feel the spirit of the
United States as the birth
of the nation is celebrated.
Each year on Pentecost
Sunday the Church
celebrates the beginning
of her work.

*What does the Church
remember on Pentecost?*

Pentecost, stained glass   (113)

Faith Focus

What happened after the Holy Spirit came on Pentecost?

Faith Vocabulary

pentecost. A word meaning "fiftieth day."

Pentecost. The feast and holy day on which the Church celebrates the coming of the Holy Spirit on the disciples.

The Festival of Weeks

People of every religion celebrate holy days. They remember and celebrate the important days of their history. The Jewish people of Jesus' time celebrated holy days too. One of these celebrations was the Festival of Weeks.

The Festival of Weeks is also known as the Festival of the First Fruits and **Pentecost**. It was called Pentecost because on the fiftieth day after Passover, the festivity and celebration began. During this festival Jewish people traveled from all over the Middle East to Jerusalem for one purpose. They came to remember and thank God for the grain harvest.

After the destruction of the Temple in Jerusalem in A.D. 70, the festival also included the celebration of God's freeing the Israelites from Egypt and giving them the Law at Sinai. This festival also came to be known as the Festival of the Giving of Law.

Think about the way people celebrate state fairs. Compare and contrast those festivals to the Festival of Weeks.

Celebrating Festivals

Different   Alike   Different

Festival of Weeks   State Fair

Pentecost

During the time of preparation for Pentecost, the disciples gathered with Mary, the Mother of Jesus, in an upper room of a home in Jerusalem. On Pentecost, the fiftieth day after Passover, the Holy Spirit came upon the disciples as Jesus had promised. Peter the Apostle and the other disciples left the room. Entering the streets, Peter proclaimed:

"[L]et the whole house of Israel know for certain that God has made [Jesus] both Lord and Messiah." . . . Now when they heard this, they were cut to the heart, and they asked Peter and the other apostles, "What are we to do, my brothers?"

Peter [said] to them, "Repent and be baptized, every one of you, in the name of Jesus Christ for the forgiveness of your sins; and you will receive the gift of the holy Spirit." . . . Those who accepted his message were baptized, and about three thousand persons were added that day.

Acts of the Apostles 2:36–38, 41

Filled with the Holy Spirit, Peter the Apostle preached the Good News of Jesus that day. The Church was born.

Imagine you are in the crowd on that first Pentecost. As Saint Peter speaks, what do you hear him saying that makes you want to become a follower of Jesus?

Peter's Message

The New Testament describes Saint Peter the Apostle beginning the work of making disciples of all nations and baptizing them as Jesus commanded the disciples to do (see Matthew 28:16–20). When Peter's listeners eagerly asked him, "What are we to do?" he responded to them very simply, "Repent and be baptized." He told them that they needed to change their hearts and believe in what God had done for them in Jesus.

The Church today continues the same work Saint Peter began on that Pentecost. The Holy Spirit invites people to change their hearts, to believe in what God has done for us in Jesus Christ. He invites people to be baptized and become disciples of Jesus.

Complete the word map. Use traits and characteristics you think helped Saint Peter do the work Jesus commanded the disciples to do. Share with a partner how the traits you named might help you tell others about Jesus.

courage

Saint Peter

Our Church Makes a Difference

Glenmary priest reading Bible stories to Vacation Bible School students in Arkansas

Glenmary Home Missioners

The Glenmary Home Missioners bring the Gospel of Jesus Christ to rural areas of Appalachia, the South, and the Southwest United States. This community of Catholic priests and brothers, joined by the Glenmary Home Mission Sisters and lay co-workers, serve people of all ages, races, and language groups.

The Glenmary Home Missioners work to build up the Catholic Church in parts of America where less than one out of every one hundred people is Catholic. They work for social justice among the poorest families in America.

In 2001 the O'Connor family decided to make their family summer vacation different. They left their home in the city and spent two weeks working with the Glenmary missioners. They were eyewitnesses of all the good that happens when we live the Gospel.

Name some of the ways a family can join the Church in telling others about Jesus.

Glenmary priest celebrating Mass in migrant camp in South Georgia

What Difference Does Faith Make in My Life?

On Pentecost the tongues of fire came to rest on Saint Peter and the other disciples. They were filled with the Holy Spirit. You have received the gift of the Holy Spirit at Baptism.

At Baptism you received the grace and responsibility to tell others about Jesus. In the two flames write ways you can share the Good News of Jesus with others.

"Go and Tell All Nations!"

_____
_____
_____
_____
_____
_____
_____

_____
_____
_____
_____
_____
_____
_____

My Faith Choice

This week I will cooperate with the Holy Spirit and join with other members of the Church to tell others about Jesus. I will

_____

_____.

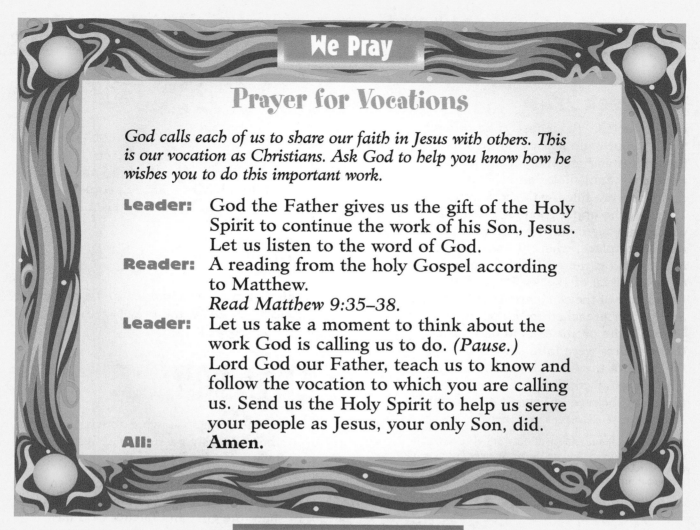

Prayer for Vocations

God calls each of us to share our faith in Jesus with others. This is our vocation as Christians. Ask God to help you know how he wishes you to do this important work.

Leader: God the Father gives us the gift of the Holy Spirit to continue the work of his Son, Jesus. Let us listen to the word of God.

Reader: A reading from the holy Gospel according to Matthew.
Read Matthew 9:35–38.

Leader: Let us take a moment to think about the work God is calling us to do. *(Pause.)*
Lord God our Father, teach us to know and follow the vocation to which you are calling us. Send us the Holy Spirit to help us serve your people as Jesus, your only Son, did.

All: **Amen.**

We Remember

Imagine you were with Saint Peter in Jerusalem on Pentecost. You are now walking home to your village. What will you share with your family and the people of your village?

_____

_____

_____

_____

_____

_____

_____

To Help You Remember

1. On Pentecost the Holy Spirit came upon the disciples as Jesus promised.

2. On Pentecost Saint Peter preached to the crowds and began the work that Jesus gave to the Church.

3. Each year on the feast of Pentecost we celebrate that the Holy Spirit helps the Church preach and teach about Jesus.

This Week . . .

In chapter 13, "Pentecost: A Scripture Story," your child learned more about the origins and meaning of the feast of Pentecost. Saint Peter and the other disciples were filled with the Holy Spirit. They left the upper room of the home where they were staying and went into the marketplace, where Jews from many nations had gathered for the celebration of the Festival of Weeks. It was the fiftieth day of the celebration, or Pentecost. Saint Peter preached to the people that in Jesus, all the promises God had made to the Israelites were fulfilled. On that day the work of the Church began. The Church today continues to invite people to repent, believe in Jesus, be baptized, and become disciples of Christ.

For more on the teachings of the Catholic Church on the Pentecost event and on the missionary mandate of the Church, see *Catechism of the Catholic Church* paragraph numbers 696, 731–732, 767, and 849–852.

Sharing God's Word

Read together Acts 2:36–41, the New Testament account of Saint Peter proclaiming Jesus to be the Lord and Messiah. Emphasize that the people believed in Jesus Christ and were baptized.

Praying

In this chapter your child learned a prayer for vocations. Read and pray together this prayer on page 119.

Making a Difference

Choose one of the following activities to do as a family or design a similar activity of your own.

- On Pentecost the Holy Spirit came to the Apostles. Invite each family member to share the gifts and talents God has given them. Talk about how they can use their gifts and talents to tell others about Jesus. Then thank God for these wonderful gifts.

- Make a mural of Pentecost, when the Holy Spirit came to the Apostles. Hang your mural where it will remind the family that the Holy Spirit is always with you.

- Name the ways the Holy Spirit helps your family. Talk about how the Holy Spirit helps you believe in Jesus and how the Holy Spirit helps you share the Good News of Jesus with others.

For more ideas on ways your family can live your faith, visit the "Faith First for Families" page at **www.FaithFirst.com**. Click on "Gospel Reflections" and talk with your family about Sunday's Gospel reading.

One Bread, One Cup

14

We Pray

I will offer a sacrifice
of thanksgiving
and call on the name
of the LORD.
PSALM 116:17

Lord, we are renewed
by the breaking
of one bread.
Help us live the new
life we received in
Baptism.   Amen.

*Imagine you are a health
expert. What foods
would you include in a
healthy meal?*

Besides food for our body,
we need food for our
spirit. At the Last Supper,
Jesus gave us his Body
and Blood to nourish our
spirit.

*Why can we call the Mass
a holy meal?*

Do This in Memory of Me

Why do we call the Mass a sacrifice?

Faith Vocabulary

Eucharist. The Sacrament of Christian Initiation in which we share in the Paschal Mystery of Christ, we receive the Body and Blood of Christ, and we are joined most fully to Christ and to the Church, the Body of Christ.

Mass. The main sacramental celebration of the Church at which we gather to listen to God's word and share in the Eucharist.

The Last Supper

The sacraments nourish and strengthen us to live as Jesus' followers. At the Last Supper Jesus gave us the sacrament of the **Eucharist.** He gave us the gift of his Body and Blood. Jesus said to his disciples, "[D]o this in memory of me" (Luke 22:19). Each time we celebrate the Eucharist, we do what Jesus did at the Last Supper.

The Sacrifice of the Cross

The next day Jesus gave up his life to save us from sin. He offered himself, or sacrificed his life, to his Father. Through the Eucharist we join in Jesus' sacrifice of his life for us. Saint Paul reminds us:

For as often as you eat this bread and drink the cup, you proclaim the death of the Lord until he comes.   1 CORINTHIANS 11:26

When we celebrate the Eucharist, we remember and share in the sacrifice of Christ. We offer ourselves with Jesus through the power of the Holy Spirit to God the Father.

Draw or write about yourself loving and serving God and others as Jesus did.

The Mystery of the Eucharist

The Eucharist is a great mystery of our faith. The Church uses many names for the Eucharist to help us understand the meaning of this great mystery of God's love.

The Lord's Supper. The Eucharist is called the Lord's Supper. We join with the Lord, the Head of the Church. We give thanks and praise to the Father as Jesus did with his disciples at the Last Supper.

Breaking of Bread. The Eucharist is the meal and banquet Jesus gave to the Church. Through the words of the priest and the power of the Holy Spirit, the unleavened bread and wine made from grapes are changed into the Body and Blood of Christ. In Holy Communion we receive the gift of Jesus himself, the Bread of Life. The consecrated bread and wine are really and truly Jesus.

The Holy Sacrifice. In the Eucharist the sacrifice of Jesus Christ is made present again. The Eucharist does not just remember and celebrate an event that has already taken place. Joined to Christ we offer ourselves through the power of the Holy Spirit to God the Father.

The Mass. The word *mass* comes from the Latin word *missio*, which means "mission" or "sending." At the conclusion of **Mass** we are sent forth on a mission. We are to "go and announce the Gospel of the Lord."

By sharing in the Eucharist we share in the fullness of life in Jesus. We are more fully joined to Jesus and to one another. We share in the Paschal Mystery of the Passion, sacrificial death, Resurrection, and glorious Ascension of Jesus Christ. We share more fully in the life of the Holy Trinity. We look forward to living forever with God and Mary and all the saints in heaven.

Talk about the sacrifices a follower of Jesus might make to live the Gospel.

The Celebration of Mass

The Church celebrates the Eucharist at Mass. The Mass is the central gathering of the Church. We come together to worship God. We join with Jesus in the power of the Holy Spirit to give thanks and praise to God the Father. Every member of the worshiping assembly has an active part in the celebration of Mass. Here are the parts, or rites, of the Mass.

The Liturgy of the Eucharist

The Eucharist is the center of our Christian life. The Liturgy of the Eucharist begins with the Preparation of the Gifts.

In the Eucharistic Prayer we join with Christ and give thanks and praise to God the Father. By the power of the Holy Spirit and the words of the priest, the bread and wine become the Body and Blood of Christ.

The whole assembly prays aloud or sings the Our Father and shares a sign of peace as we prepare for Holy Communion. We profess our faith in Jesus Christ, the Lamb of God who takes away the sins of the world. We walk in procession to receive the Body and Blood of Christ.

The Introductory Rites

We remember and celebrate that God has called us together to be his people. We gather and form a worshiping community, which we call the worshiping assembly.

The Liturgy of the Word

The Sunday celebration of Mass includes three Scripture readings. We listen and respond to God's word. The Gospel reading, which is the third reading, is the center of the Liturgy of the Word. After the proclamation of the Gospel, the priest or deacon preaches a homily. This helps us understand and live the word of God. We then pray the Profession of Faith, or Creed, and the Prayer of the Faithful.

The Concluding Rites

The priest asks God's blessing on the assembly. We are sent forth to carry on the work, or mission, of Jesus Christ.

Write why the Eucharist is the center of your life as a Catholic.

_____

_____

_____

_____

_____

Our Church Makes a Difference

Blessed Teresa of Calcutta, the Saint of the Gutter

Blessed Mother Teresa of Calcutta loved and served the Lord through her love and service of the poorest of the poor. She wrote, "I see God in every human being. When I wash the leper's wounds, I feel that I am nursing the Lord himself."

The Eucharist was the center of Mother Teresa's life. Every day she took part in the Mass and shared the Eucharist. At the conclusion of the celebration of Mass, she heard the words, "Go in peace to love and serve the Lord." Because of her work with people who were left to die on the streets, Mother Teresa became known as the Saint of the Gutter.

Beatification ceremony of Mother Teresa at the Vatican, Sunday, October 19, 2003

Mother Teresa received the Nobel Peace Prize in 1979. In 1985 she was awarded the Medal of Freedom by the president of the United States. On the night she died, the president of France said, "This evening, there is less love, less compassion, less light in the world." These and other honors recognized the difference Blessed Mother Teresa's life made for the world.

On October 19, 2003, just six years after she died, Pope John Paul II named Mother Teresa a Blessed of the Church. This honor recognizes that Mother Teresa faithfully lived the Gospel and is a model for all of us to follow.

Our Catholic Identity

Blessed Sacrament

The consecrated bread, which is the Body of Christ, is called the Blessed Sacrament. We reserve the Blessed Sacrament in the tabernacle for those who are sick and for the devotion of the people.

How does the Eucharist help you show your love for God and for others?

Tapestry of Mother Teresa displayed at her Beatification ceremony

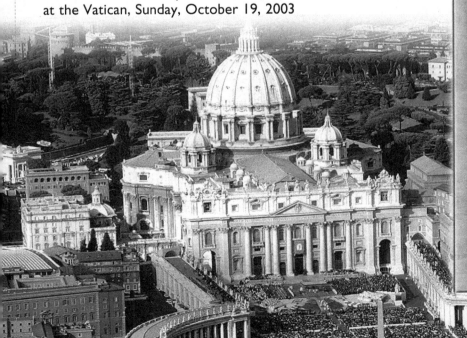

What Difference Does Faith Make in My Life?

The Eucharist is the center of the Christian life. Receiving the Eucharist strengthens you "to love and serve the Lord."

Describe how you can love and serve the Lord.

Serving the Lord

Home: _____
_____
_____.

School: _____
_____
_____.

Neighborhood: _____
_____
_____.

My Faith Choice

This week through my acts and words I will love and serve the Lord by

_____
_____.

Sacrament Most Holy

Each year on the second Sunday after Pentecost we celebrate the Solemnity of the Most Holy Body and Blood of Christ. After the second reading we may pray aloud or sing the hymn Lauda Sion. We praise God for the gift of the Eucharist.

Leader: Let us give thanks and praise to God for the gift of the Eucharist.

Group 1: The cup of blessing that we bless is the blood of Christ.

All: Bring God all the praise you know.

Group 2: The bread we break is the body of Christ.

All: Bring God all the praise you know.

Group 3: Whoever eats the bread and drinks from the cup will live forever.

All: Bring God all the praise you know.

BASED ON 1 CORINTHIANS 10:16–17, JOHN 6:51, AND LAUDA SION

We Remember

Complete this crossword puzzle. Each clue for the puzzle points to the mystery of the Eucharist.

To Help You Remember

1. Jesus gave us the Eucharist at the Last Supper.

2. The celebration of the Eucharist renews and makes present the one sacrifice of Christ.

3. Through the Eucharist we share in the death and Resurrection of Christ.

DOWN

1. The _____ is the central celebration of the Church.
3. By sharing in the _____ we share in the fullness of life in Jesus.
4. The parts of the Mass are called _____.
5. In Holy Communion we receive _____.

ACROSS

2. The _____ bread, which is the Body of Christ, is called the Blessed Sacrament.
6. When we celebrate the Eucharist we join in Jesus' _____ of his life for us.

This Week . . .

In chapter 14, "One Bread, One Cup," your child learned more about the sacrament of the Eucharist. The Eucharist is at the center of the Christian life. It is the sacrament of the Body and Blood of the Lord Jesus Christ. At the Eucharist the bread and wine truly become the Body and Blood of Christ through the power of the Holy Spirit and the words of the priest. When we celebrate the Eucharist, the sacrifice of Jesus Christ is made present. We share in the Paschal Mystery of the Passion, death, Resurrection, and glorious Ascension of Christ and receive the promise of eternal life.

For more on the teachings of the Catholic Church on the sacrament of the Eucharist, see *Catechism of the Catholic Church* paragraph numbers 1322–1405.

Sharing God's Word

Read together 1 Corinthians 11:23–26, Saint Paul's account of the institution of the Eucharist. Emphasize that on the day after the Last Supper Jesus offered his life on the cross.

Praying

In this chapter your child prayed a prayer praising God for the gift of the Eucharist. Read and pray together this prayer on page 127.

Making a Difference

Choose one of the following activities to do as a family or design a similar activity of your own.

- *Reverence* is another word for *respect*. Talk about all the ways to show reverence for the Eucharist during Mass.

- When your family takes part in the celebration of Mass this week, spend some time after Mass at the tabernacle. You will notice a candle burning next to the tabernacle. This candle is called a sanctuary lamp. Genuflect before the tabernacle to show your reverence and respect for the Blessed Sacrament.

- At the end of Mass, the assembly is sent forth with these or similar words: "Go in peace, glorifying the Lord by your life." All respond, "Amen." Choose one thing you can do this week to love and serve the Lord. All respond, "Thanks be to God."

For more ideas on ways your family can live your faith, visit the "Faith First for Families" page at **www.FaithFirst.com**. Click on "Make a Difference" for ideas of ways your family can share God's love with others this week.

The Corinthians
A Scripture Story

15

We Pray

LORD, you are the strength
  of your people. . . .
Save your people, bless
  your inheritance;
  feed and sustain them
  forever!   PSALM 28:8–9

**Lord God, Father
of all, may sharing
in the Body and Blood
of Christ, your Son,
join all your people
in love.   Amen.**

*What is one thing you know
about your family's history?*

Learning our family history
helps us understand who
we are. One thing we
learn about the history of
our Church is that we
have always gathered to
celebrate the Eucharist.

*Why do we celebrate the
Eucharist?*

The Eucharist, stained glass   (129)

Bible Background

Faith Focus

What does Saint Paul's First Letter to the Corinthians tell us about the Eucharist?

Faith Vocabulary

epistle. A type of formal letter found in the New Testament.

breaking of bread. A name used for the celebration of the Eucharist.

The Church at Corinth

The first followers of Jesus were Jewish people who asked to be baptized. Many non-Jews, or Gentiles, who were living in towns and cities all around the Mediterranean Sea also became followers of Jesus. Corinth, a city in ancient Greece, was one of these cities.

Saint Paul, who is known as the Apostle to the Gentiles, preached the Gospel to the people of Corinth. He first came to Corinth in A.D. 51, about twenty years after Jesus' death, Resurrection, and Ascension. Paul stayed there about a year and a half preaching the Gospel. Many Corinthians came to believe in Jesus Christ and asked to be baptized.

After Paul preached in Corinth, he traveled by land and sea to other cities. Because Paul could not always travel back to the cities he had already visited, he wrote letters, sometimes called **epistles**, to them.

Design a home page for your parish Web site. Make your parish celebration of the Eucharist the center of your design.

Reading the Word of God

The Lord's Supper

When Saint Paul was in the city of Ephesus, he learned about the Corinthians' lack of reverence and respect for the Eucharist. He wrote:

> I hear that when you meet as a church there are divisions among you. . . . When you meet in one place, then, it is not to eat the Lord's supper, for in eating, each one goes ahead with his own supper, and one goes hungry while another gets drunk.
>
> 1 Corinthians 11:18, 20–21

Then Paul explained to the Corinthians the true meaning of the Eucharist.

He reminded them that they were doing what Jesus did at the Last Supper. They were sharing in the Body and Blood of Christ. He wrote:

> Therefore, whoever eats the bread or drinks the cup of the Lord unworthily will have to answer for the body and blood of the Lord. A person should examine himself, and so eat the bread and drink the cup.
>
> 1 Corinthians 11:27–28

Saint Paul helped the Corinthians understand that when they came together for the **breaking of bread**, they were sharing the Body and Blood of the Lord.

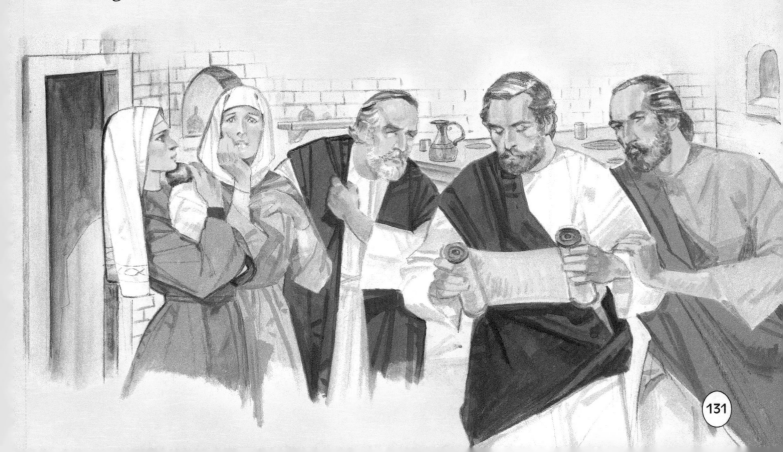

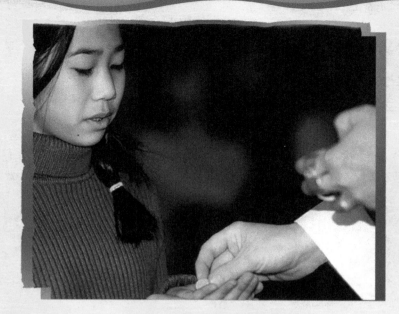

The Eucharist Today

Saint Paul reprimanded the Corinthians for their lack of reverence during the celebration of the Eucharist. They were arguing and quarreling. They divided themselves into hostile groups. Some were even getting drunk. Their words and actions did not show that they understood they were sharing the Body and Blood of Christ.

Paul told the Corinthians that their behavior—their words and actions—needed to show that they understood what they were doing. They were making present and sharing in the loving sacrifice of Jesus. They were not eating bread and drinking wine. They were sharing the Body and Blood of Christ shed for the sins of the world.

When we celebrate the Eucharist, we too need to remember Paul's words. We are sharing in the Body and Blood of Christ. Our words and actions are to express our faith that Jesus is with us.

Write how you might prepare to take part properly in the Eucharist.

_____

_____

_____

_____

_____

Our Catholic Identity

Roman Missal and Lectionary

The Roman Missal is a book that contains all the prayers for the celebration of the Mass. The Lectionary is the book that contains the three-year cycle of Scripture readings for the Mass.

Pope John Paul II, signing an encyclical, an official letter teaching about the faith

Church Letters

The Church is our teacher. The pope and other bishops share in the responsibility Jesus gave the Apostles to teach in his name. The pope and the bishops, as Saint Paul did, sometimes teach us by writing letters.

The Church today writes different kinds of letters. One type of letter the pope writes is called an apostolic letter. On Pentecost 1998, Pope John Paul II sent the apostolic letter "The Day of the Lord" to all the bishops to share with the people they serve.

In his letter Pope John Paul II teaches that celebrating the Eucharist together as the Church is the heart of Sunday. Sunday is the Lord's Day. Resting from our work and other chores on Sunday helps us show our reverence for God the Creator and devote time to our families and to ourselves. When we keep Sunday holy, we build up not only the Church but also our families and communities too.

What are some ways the Church helps people make the Lord's Day special?

133

What Difference Does Faith Make in My Life?

Every Sunday you go to church and take part in the Eucharist. There are many things you do and say that show reverence for the Eucharist.

Pretend you have been invited to help a first grader act reverently and attentively at Mass. In the space below write what you would say.

My Faith Choice

 This week I will think about what is really happening when I take part in the Eucharist. To celebrate more attentively and reverently I will

_____

_____.

The Divine Praises

At the celebration of Benediction of the Blessed Sacrament the Church prays the Divine Praises. Pray this part of the Divine Praises. Bless and praise God the Father for the gift of Jesus.

Leader: Let us bless and praise God the Father for the gift of Jesus present with us as the Blessed Sacrament.
Blessed be Jesus Christ, true God and true man.

All: **Blessed be Jesus Christ, true God and true man.**

Leader: Blessed be the name of Jesus.

All: **Blessed be the name of Jesus.**

Leader: Blessed be his most Sacred Heart.

All: **Blessed be his most Sacred Heart.**

Leader: Blessed be his most precious Blood.

All: **Blessed be his most precious Blood.**

Leader: Blessed be Jesus in the most holy Sacrament of the altar.

All: **Blessed be Jesus in the most holy Sacrament of the altar.**

We Remember

Write a sentence describing these words and phrases.

1. epistle _____

_____

2. breaking of bread _____

_____

3. Lord's Supper _____

_____

To Help You Remember

1. The early Church met in homes for the breaking of the bread.

2. Saint Paul wrote to the Corinthians reminding them that when they celebrated the Eucharist, they were sharing in the Lord's Supper.

3. When we celebrate the Eucharist we are to celebrate it in a way that shows we truly believe we share the Body and Blood of the Lord.

This Week . . .

In chapter 15, "The Corinthians: A Scripture Story," your child learned about the Eucharist. Saint Paul the Apostle established many Christian communities on his missionary journeys. Among those communities was the Christian community in the seaport town of Corinth in ancient Greece. After Paul left Corinth, he wrote to the Corinthians from Ephesus to remind them that their words and actions must show their belief in the Eucharist. Our words and actions at the Eucharist must express our faith that Jesus is with us in the Eucharist.

For more on the teachings of the Catholic Church on the Eucharist as the Lord's Supper and the breaking of bread, see *Catechism of the Catholic Church* paragraph numbers 1328–1329.

Sharing God's Word

Read together 1 Corinthians 11:18–28. Emphasize that Saint Paul reminded the Corinthians that the Eucharist is the Body and Blood of Christ.

Praying

In this chapter your child prayed the Divine Praises. Read and pray together this prayer on page 135.

Making a Difference

Choose one of the following activities to do as a family or design a similar activity of your own.

- Invite each family member to share what they can remember about their First Communion day. Talk about how old they were, who was present, how they felt, and so on.

- Write a letter in your own words about the Eucharist. Include the significance of sharing in the Body and Blood of Christ regularly.

- Talk about how your words and actions show that the Eucharist, the Body and Blood, is Jesus.

For more ideas on ways your family can live your faith, visit the "Faith First for Families" page at **www.FaithFirst.com**. Check out "Bible Stories." Read and discuss the Bible story as a family this week.

Jesus' Work of Healing

16

We Pray

Bless the LORD, my soul;
  do not forget all the
    gifts of God,
Who pardons all
    your sins,
  heals all your ills.

PSALM 103:2–3

Lord God,
share your mercy and
love with all who call
on you.   Amen.

*Why is it important to
forgive and be forgiven?
Why is it important to help
people who are sick?*

Forgiveness and healing
are a part of our daily
lives. Jesus continues his
work of forgiveness and
healing through the
Sacraments of Healing.

*What are the Sacraments
of Healing?*

137

Faith Focus

What do we celebrate in the Sacraments of Healing?

Faith Vocabulary

Penance and Reconciliation. The Sacrament of Healing through which we receive God's forgiveness through the ministry of the priest for the sins we commit after Baptism.

Anointing of the Sick. The Sacrament of Healing that strengthens our faith, hope, and love for God when we are seriously ill, weakened by old age, or dying.

Our Need for God's Forgiveness

Everyone needs forgiveness. Everyone needs to forgive. God is always ready to forgive us when we sin. Sin is freely choosing to do or say what we know is against God's will. Sin shows disrespect for God. There is no greater evil than sin. When we sin, we harm, or hurt, the person God created us to be. We offend God and harm other people and the community of the Church. When we sin we also show disrespect for ourselves. We wound our human dignity. We need God's help, or grace, not to sin again.

The Holy Spirit invites us to ask for and accept God's forgiveness. The Spirit also helps us change our ways and live more like children of God.

Through the Sacrament of **Penance and Reconciliation**, we receive both God's forgiveness for the sins we commit after Baptism and his grace not to sin. Jesus gave the Church this sacrament (see John 20:22–23). Today bishops and priests speak in the name of Jesus when they offer God's forgiveness. Through the words of the bishop or priest and the power of the Holy Spirit, our sins are forgiven in this sacrament. We are reconciled, or made friends again, with God and the Church.

Create a brief prayer. Thank God for the gift of his forgiveness.

_____

_____

_____

_____

_____

_____

Penance and Reconciliation

When we celebrate the sacrament of Penance and Reconciliation, we share in God's forgiving and healing love. We can celebrate this sacrament alone with the priest or we can gather as a community and celebrate it. As God forgives us, we too are to forgive all those who sin against us. We need to learn ways to ask for forgiveness and to forgive others. When we forgive, we bring healing to others. When we are forgiven, we receive the gift of healing. We must treat others the same way we ask God to treat us. These four things are always part of the celebration of the sacrament of Penance and Reconciliation.

The Rite of Reconciliation

Confession of sins

We meet individually with a priest and confess, or tell, our sins to him. We always confess any serious sins.

Contrition for sins

We pray an act of contrition. In this prayer we admit we have sinned. We express our sorrow for having offended God. Being truly sorry for our sins means we do not want to sin again. We really want to cooperate with the Holy Spirit to change the way we live.

Penance

The priest gives us a penance. He may ask us to say a prayer or do an act of kindness. Accepting and doing our penance shows that we are truly sorry for our sins and that we want to make up for the harm caused by our sins.

Absolution

Absolution is the forgiveness that the priest speaks in the name of God. When the priest says, "I absolve you," God speaks through him. *I absolve you* means "I forgive you. You are free from your sins."

Think about one time someone forgave you. Think about one time you forgave someone. How did it feel to be forgiven? How did it feel to forgive?

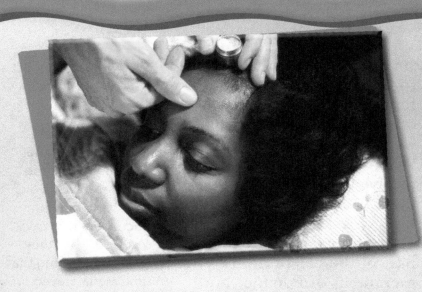

them spiritually. Each time Jesus not only healed their bodies but, more importantly, he helped them grow in faith, trust, and love for God.

Christ gave the Church the sacrament of the **Anointing of the Sick** to continue his work among the sick in the world. The Church celebrates this sacrament with members of the Church who are seriously ill or weak because of old age. Through union with Jesus, the sick find strength, peace, and courage. Christ's sufferings give a new meaning to our suffering.

Anointing of the Sick

Jesus sometimes cured people of their sickness. He cured the man born blind (see John 9:1–12) and he cured the paralyzed man (see Mark 2:5–11). When Jesus healed people who were sick, he also healed

Rite of Anointing of the Sick

Only a priest or bishop can administer this sacrament. He meets and prays with the sick or elderly person and with their family and those caring for them. Next he reads from the word of God. Then he leads the celebration of the Liturgy of Anointing. These are the main parts of the celebration.

Litany, or Prayer of Faith

The priest leads all present, who represent the whole Church, in a prayer of faith in response to God's word.

Laying on of hands

Jesus often laid his hands on sick people (see Luke 4:40). The Church uses this same gesture in this sacrament. It shows that the Church is asking God's blessing on the sick person.

Anointing with oil

The priest or bishop anoints the sick person with the oil of the sick. First he anoints the sick person's forehead, as he prays, "Through this holy anointing may the Lord in his love and mercy help you with the grace of the Holy Spirit." Then he anoints the person's hands as he prays, "May the Lord who frees you from sin save you and raise you up."

With a partner discuss ways you might continue Christ's work among the sick.

Our Church Makes a Difference

Catholic Hospitals

From the very beginning of the Church, caring for the sick has been an important ministry of the Church. Catholic hospitals continue this tradition. Each year more than seventy-one million patients are cared for in over a thousand Catholic hospitals and health-care centers in the United States.

The hospitals are often named after saints, such as Saint Frances Cabrini, who dedicated their lives to caring for the sick. The names of hospitals sometimes reflect the healing stories of Jesus, such as Good Samaritan Hospital and Mercy Hospital.

A Catholic hospital is a symbol that the Church continues the work of Christ the Healer in towns, cities, and countries all over the world. The work of Catholic hospitals reminds us that all the baptized share in the healing work of Christ.

What are some of the ways your parish continues Jesus' work of healing with people who are sick?

Our Catholic Identity

Chaplains

A chaplain sometimes serves a hospital. A chaplain can be a priest, deacon, or layperson. Hospital chaplains are trained to participate in the healing mission of Christ. They not only minister to the sick but also spiritually support hospital workers. Parish ministers to the sick often work with chaplains.

Guardian angel protecting boy. Mural on exterior of Christus Rosa Hospital, San Antonio, Texas.

Medical emergency transport helicopter

What Difference Does Faith Make in My Life?

The Holy Spirit helps you continue the healing work of Jesus. You forgive those who may offend you. You reach out to family, friends, and neighbors when they are sick.

Create a title and design a cover for this music CD. Include two song titles. Choose titles that remind people of God's healing love with people.

My Faith Choice

This week I will continue the healing work of Jesus. I will

_____

_____.

A Prayer for the Sick

When we pray for other people we pray a prayer of intercession.
Pray this prayer of intercession for people who are sick.

Leader: Jesus showed us God's love for people
who are sick.
Let us pray to God for all the members
of our families, for our friends, and
for all who are sick. *(Pause.)*
Bless those who are sick and fill them
with new hope and strength.

All: **Lord, have mercy.**

Leader: Support all those who care for the sick.

All: **Lord, have mercy.**

Leader: Quietly give thanks to
God who is full of
mercy and kindness.

We Remember

*Circle T if the statement is true. Circle F if the
statement is false. Make the false statements true.*

1. Penance and Reconciliation and
Anointing of the Sick are Sacraments
of Service.　　　　　　　　　　　T　F

2. Another name for the sacrament
of Penance and Reconciliation is
the sacrament of Reconciliation.　T　F

3. Confession, contrition, penance, and
absolution are all part of the sacrament
of Penance and Reconciliation.　T　F

4. The Church celebrates Anointing of the
Sick with young people, grown-ups,
and elderly people.　　　　　　T　F

5. All the baptized can administer the
sacrament of Anointing of the Sick.　T　F

To Help You Remember

1. The sacraments of Penance
and Reconciliation and
Anointing of the Sick
continue Jesus' ministry
of healing.

2. Through Reconciliation we
are forgiven the sins we
commit after we are
baptized.

3. Through Anointing of the
Sick those who are seriously
ill, weakened because of old
age, or dying are joined to
the suffering of Christ and
receive strength and
courage.

This Week . . .

In chapter 16, "Jesus' Work of Healing," your child learned more about the two Sacraments of Healing: Reconciliation and Anointing of the Sick. Through Reconciliation we receive forgiveness for sins we commit after Baptism. Confession of sins, contrition (or sorrow), penance, and absolution are always a part of the rite of Reconciliation. Throughout his life on earth Jesus also cured people of body illnesses. When he did so he also reached out to heal their spirits and invite people to grow in faith, trust, and love for God. Through Anointing of the Sick, Christ continues his healing ministry among the sick in the world today.

For more on the teachings of the Catholic Church on the Sacraments of Healing, see *Catechism of the Catholic Church* paragraph numbers 1420–1484 and 1499–1525.

Sharing God's Word

Read together John 20:22–23. Emphasize that bishops and priests today speak in the name of Jesus when they offer God's forgiveness in the sacrament of Reconciliation, or Penance.

Praying

In this chapter your child prayed a prayer for the sick. Read and pray together this prayer on page 143.

Making a Difference

Choose one of the following activities to do as a family or design a similar activity of your own.

- Invite family members to share stories about forgiving others and being forgiven. Emphasize that when we forgive, we bring healing to others. When we are forgiven, we receive the gift of healing.

- Talk about all the ways your parish continues the healing work of Jesus.

- Talk about how your family continues the healing work of Jesus. Choose one thing you will do this week to continue the healing work of Jesus.

For more ideas on ways your family can live your faith, visit the "Faith First for Families" page at **www.FaithFirst.com**. You will find it helpful to take a look at "Questions Kids Ask."

Called to Serve the Whole Church

We Pray

Praise the LORD, my soul;
I shall praise the LORD
all my life,
sing praise to my God
while I live.

PSALM 146:2

Father, give those
who serve the Church
the strength to be
witnesses of Christ,
your Son, to others.

Amen.

Who are some people who serve others in your family, school, or parish?

People work together in families, in schools, in communities. The sacraments of Holy Orders and Matrimony call and strengthen some members of the Church to serve the whole Church.

In what ways do those who receive Holy Orders and Matrimony serve the Church?

Exchange of Rings, stained glass

145

Serving the Whole Church

Faith Focus

What do the Sacraments at the Service of Communion celebrate?

Faith Vocabulary

Holy Orders. The Sacrament at the Service of Communion through which a baptized man is consecrated to serve the whole Church as a bishop, priest, or deacon.

Matrimony. The Sacrament at the Service of Communion that unites a baptized man and a baptized woman in a lifelong bond, or covenant, of faithful love to serve the Church as a sign of Christ's love for the Church.

Our Christian Vocation

Baptism joins us to Christ and to all the members of the Church. We receive the call, or vocation, and grace to continue the work of Christ, to build up the Church, and to seek the kingdom of God.

All the baptized, laypeople, religious, and ordained ministers are members of the Body of Christ. Saint Paul the Apostle reminds us that each member has an important role in the Church (see 1 Corinthians 12:12–30).

The two sacraments of **Holy Orders** and **Matrimony** consecrate, or set aside for a holy purpose, members of the Church to serve the whole Church. Because these two sacraments set aside for a holy purpose some members of the Church to serve the whole Church, they are called Sacraments at the Service of Communion.

Write how you see a married couple serving the Church.

_____

_____

_____

_____

_____

_____

Holy Orders

In Holy Orders a baptized man is ordained as a bishop, priest, or deacon to serve the whole Church. Only bishops can ordain other bishops, priests, and deacons.

Bishops share in the fullness of Christ's priesthood and continue the work of the Apostles. They proclaim and preach God's word, lead us in celebrating the sacraments, and guide us in living the Gospel.

Priests are coworkers with their bishop. They preach God's word and lead us in the celebration of the sacraments. Priests stand for Christ and speak in his name.

Deacons help the bishops and priests. They proclaim God's word and can baptize and marry people. Sometimes they are married themselves. Deacons often minister to the sick and those in need.

Describe the ways that bishops, priests, and deacons are serving the Church.

Rite of Ordination of a Priest

Laying on of hands. In silence, the ordaining bishop lays his hands on the heads of the candidates to be ordained. Next, all the priests who are present do the same.

Prayer of consecration. The ordaining bishop prays the prayer of consecration. He prays, in part, "Almighty Father, grant to these servants of yours the dignity of the priesthood."

Investiture with stole and chasuble. Each of the newly ordained priests receives a stole and a chasuble and puts them on.

Anointing of hands. The palms of the hands of the newly ordained are anointed with chrism as the bishop prays, "The Father anointed our Lord Jesus Christ through the power of the Holy Spirit. May Jesus preserve you to sanctify the Christian people to offer sacrifice to God."

Matrimony

God created man and woman to be together. He created them to marry, share God's love with each other, and bring children into the world. Marriage is a sign of God's faithful and life-giving love for all people.

Matrimony is the name the Church gives to the sacrament of marriage. Matrimony unites a baptized man and a baptized woman in marriage and makes the couple a sign of Christ's love for the Church.

The Christian couple who marry are closer to each other than to anyone else. They form a new family in the Church. In the sacrament of Matrimony, they receive the grace to live their vocation as a sign of Christ's love for the Church and of God's love for all people.

Using each letter in the word LOVE, create a phrase or sentence that tells how the members of a Christian family can be a sign of Christ's love for us.

L _____

_____

O _____

_____

V _____

_____

E _____

_____

Rite of Marriage

The celebration of Matrimony can take place during Mass or outside of Mass. The celebration of the sacrament takes place right after the Liturgy of the Word. This is what happens during the celebration of the sacrament.

- The bride and groom individually tell the priest or deacon and everyone present they are marrying freely.
- They promise that they will love and honor each other and will be faithful to each other as husband and wife until they die.
- They promise to accept the children God will give them and to raise them according to God's Law.
- They usually give each other a ring to wear as a sign of their love and commitment to each other.
- The priest asks God to bless the newly married couple.

Our Church Makes a Difference

Working Together as a Parish

All the people in a parish—the ordained, the married, the single, and the members of religious communities—are called to share their time and talents with others. All have the responsibility to take part in the work of the Church.

Adults serve the parish in many ways. Some work on the parish council and help organize the work of the parish. Some read the Scriptures at Mass, serve as extraordinary ministers of Holy Communion, or teach as catechists. Others are sponsors of those who want to become Catholics. Some take care of parish buildings or work with fund-raisers that help the parish do its work.

Some adults in the parish care for those who are sick or elderly. Others help people who are in financial difficulties or have lost their jobs. Others work with organizations in the community to build and repair houses. Some volunteer to serve people who are homeless. A few work with government leaders to get laws passed that help build a more just and fair community. The members of a parish give witness to Jesus through their work in the world. They prepare the way for the coming of the kingdom of God announced by Jesus.

When do you see the members of your parish helping one another live as followers of Jesus Christ?

What Difference Does Faith Make in My Life?

God calls you to serve others. The things you are doing now to help others are preparing you to continue serving the Church when you grow up.

Choose one talent God has blessed you with. Write it in the center circle. Then around the outside circle name ways you can use this talent to serve the Church.

Serving the Church

My Faith Choice

This week I will work with others to do the work of the Church. I will

_____

_____.

We Pray

Love One Another

Praying the Scripture guides us in living our faith. Join in praying this service of the word.

Leader: Jesus taught us what it means to serve people.
We are to love others as he loves us.

Reader: A reading from the Letter to the Colossians. *(Read Colossians 3:12–15.)*
The word of the Lord.

All: **Thanks be to God.**

Leader: Let us ask the Holy Spirit to teach us ways to serve others as Jesus taught us to do. *(Pause.)*
Now let us share a sign of peace with one another.

We Remember

List three reasons why the sacraments of Holy Orders and Matrimony are called Sacraments at the Service of Communion.

1. _____
   _____
   _____

2. _____
   _____
   _____

3. _____
   _____
   _____

To Help You Remember

1. Matrimony and Holy Orders consecrate, or set aside for a holy purpose, some members of the Church to serve the whole Church.

2. Holy Orders is the sacrament in which a baptized man is consecrated to serve the whole Church as a bishop, priest, or deacon by continuing the work Jesus gave the Apostles.

3. Matrimony is the sacrament that unites a baptized man and a baptized woman in a lifelong bond, or covenant, of faithful love to serve the Church as a sign of Christ's love for the Church.

This Week . . .

In chapter 17, "Called to Serve the Whole Church," your child learned that God calls some members of the Church to serve the whole Church. Through Holy Orders bishops, priests, and deacons are ordained to serve the whole Church by continuing the unique work Jesus entrusted to the Apostles. Through Matrimony a baptized man and a baptized woman are united in a lifelong bond, or covenant, of faithful love and become a sign of Christ's love for the Church. These sacraments, which are Holy Orders and Matrimony, are called Sacraments at the Service of Communion.

For more on the teachings of the Catholic Church on the Sacraments at the Service of Communion, see *Catechism of the Catholic Church* paragraph numbers 1533–1589 and 1601–1658.

Sharing God's Word

Read together 1 Corinthians 12:12–30. Emphasize that each member of the Church has an important role as a member of the Body of Christ.

Praying

In this chapter your child prayed the Scriptures. Read and pray together this prayer on page 151.

Making a Difference

Choose one of the following activities to do as a family or design a similar activity of your own.

• Invite family members to share one talent that God has given them. Then ask each person to share how they can use this talent to live as a follower of Christ.

• When you take part in Mass this week, look in the parish bulletin. Find all the ways your parish helps one another live as followers of Christ.

• Talk about the work that Matrimony and Holy Orders set aside married couples, bishops, priests, and deacons to do. Name ways that married couples and priests are signs of Christ's love. Then choose one way your family can be a sign of Christ's love.

For more ideas on ways your family can live your faith, visit the "Faith First for Families" page at **www.FaithFirst.com**. Click on "Family Prayer" and pray the prayer of the week.

Unit 2 Review

Name _____

A. Best Response

Read each statement and circle the best answer.

1. What is the Liturgy of the Church?
   a. the Church's work of worshiping God
   b. the work of helping others
   c. the gifts of the Holy Spirit
   d. the work of living the Beatitudes

2. Which season of the Church's liturgical year celebrates the Resurrection and our new life in Christ?
   a. Lent
   b. Ordinary Time
   c. Advent
   d. Easter

3. Which one of the following is not a Sacrament of Initiation?
   a. Confirmation
   b. Eucharist
   c. Penance and Reconciliation
   d. Baptism

4. Which of the following is not an effect of Baptism?
   a. We receive new life in Jesus Christ.
   b. We become members of the Body of Christ, the Church.
   c. We are freed from original sin and all personal sins.
   d. We receive the Body and Blood of Christ.

5. Which sacrament completes our Baptism?
   a. Anointing of the Sick
   b. Confirmation
   c. Matrimony
   d. Penance and Reconciliation

6. What happened on the first Pentecost?
   a. The disciples prayed with Jesus.
   b. Jesus healed Jairus's daughter.
   c. Jesus was baptized.
   d. The Holy Spirit came upon the Apostles.

7. When did Jesus give us the sacrament of the Eucharist?
   a. at the wedding feast of Cana
   b. on the feast of Pentecost
   c. at the Last Supper
   d. at the Crucifixion

8. Why do we gather to celebrate Mass?
   a. to do a penance
   b. to receive absolution
   c. to give thanks and praise to God the Father
   d. to be anointed with oil

9. Which one of the following is not a part of the sacrament of Penance and Reconciliation?
   a. confession of sins
   b. doing a penance
   c. contrition for sins
   d. anointing with oil

10. Which of the following are the Sacraments at the Service of Communion?
    a. Baptism and Holy Orders
    b. Holy Orders and Matrimony
    c. Penance and Reconciliation and Anointing of the Sick
    d. Matrimony and Confirmation

B. Words and Phrases

Match the terms in column A with their descriptions in column B.

Column A

_____ 1. Triduum

_____ 2. Lent

_____ 3. Mass

_____ 4. Pentecost

_____ 5. sacrifice

_____ 6. epistles

_____ 7. Corinth

_____ 8. Eucharist

Column B

a. the Lord's Supper

b. Jesus dying to save us from sin

c. comes from the Latin word meaning "mission"

d. letters written by Saint Paul and others

e. a city in ancient Greece with followers of Jesus

f. the Holy Spirit coming upon the disciples

g. six weeks of preparation for Easter

h. Holy Thursday, Good Friday, and Easter Vigil

C. What I Have Learned

Name three things you learned in this unit.
Share them with the group.

_____

_____

_____

Look at the list of faith terms on page 96.
Circle the ones you know now.

D. From a Scripture Story

Saint Paul reminded the Corinthians of the true meaning
of the Eucharist. Use words or drawings to complete the following.

Saint Paul's Teaching about the Eucharist	What Happens at the Eucharist

How do we live a life of holiness?

Getting Ready

What I Have Learned

What is something you already know about these faith terms?

Conscience

_____

_____

The Beatitudes

_____

_____

Holiness

_____

_____

Words to Know

Put an X next to the faith terms you know. Put a ? next to the faith terms you need to know more about.

Faith Vocabulary

_____ moral decisions

_____ Sermon on the Mount

_____ grace

_____ actual grace

_____ the catholic letters

_____ Ten Commandments

_____ the Covenant

_____ chastity

_____ justice

Questions I Have

What questions would you like to ask about God's gift of grace?

_____

_____

_____

_____

A Scripture Story

John's message of God's love

How do you show God's love?

Making Christian Decisions

We Pray

Make known to me
   your ways, LORD;
teach me your paths.
PSALM 25:4

Lord God, make us
ready to live the
Gospel and eager
to do your will. Amen.

*What are some decisions
you make every day?*

Every day you make
choices and decisions.
Your choices tell people
a lot about you. Think
about some of the
decisions you have made.

*How do you know if your
decision is a good one?*

Choosing to Live a Holy Life

Faith Focus

Why is it important to make good moral decisions?

Faith Vocabulary

moral decisions.
The decisions and choices we make to live as children of God and followers of Jesus Christ.

conscience. The gift of God that is part of every person and that guides us to know and judge what is right and wrong.

Choosing What Is Good

God made us to know him, to love him, and to serve him. **Moral decisions** are the choices we make to live as children of God and followers of Christ. They bring us closer to living the life that God created us to live. They build up our relationship with God, the Church, and others. Moral decisions strengthen our character and lead us toward the happiness God created us to have. Our intellect, free will, and feelings can help us make moral decisions.

Intellect. Our intellect gives us the ability to learn more and more about God, ourselves, others, and the world in which we live.

Free will. Our free will is the power God gives us to make our own decisions. We can choose to do what we know is good or evil.

Feelings. Our feelings, or emotions, are neither good nor bad. They can help us do good or they can weaken us to do evil.

Sadly, we live in a world in which original sin has weakened our intellect and will. We do not always use our feelings to help us choose what we know is good. We struggle to overcome temptation. Temptation is everything that moves us to make decisions that lead us away from living as children of God.

The Holy Spirit always helps and guides us to make good decisions and to overcome temptation. We just need to remember to ask for help.

On a separate piece of paper design a note card with a phrase that can help you and others remember to make moral decisions. Keep your card where you will see it often.

The Gift of Conscience

Every person is born with a gift that helps us make moral decisions. This gift is our **conscience**. Our conscience guides us to know and judge what is right and what is wrong.

Just as we develop our gifts to play a sport, do math, use computers, play a musical instrument, or dance or sing, we also need to develop our ability to make moral decisions. Here are some ways we can develop or train our conscience.

- Pray to the Holy Spirit.
- Take part in the celebration of the sacraments, especially the Eucharist and Reconciliation.
- Read, study, and pray the Bible, especially the Gospels.
- Study what the Church teaches about how we should live.
- Learn from the lives of others, such as the saints, who have lived holy lives.
- Ask the advice of our parents and other adults who teach us about our faith.

Our ability to use and follow our conscience can also become weakened. We can develop a bad conscience. It is very important that we work hard at forming a good conscience. This is something we have the responsibility to do all of our lives.

You have read about six ways you can train your conscience. Choose one of these ways and make a plan of how you will use it to train your conscience.

Forming a Good Conscience

The Four Cardinal Virtues

The more we train our voice to sing or practice our serve in tennis, the more improvement we see. We develop good habits, or ways of doing things that seem natural. The same is true in following a well-trained conscience and making moral decisions. The more we cooperate with the grace of the Holy Spirit and work at making moral decisions, the better we become at it. We develop moral virtues.

The moral virtues are spiritual powers, or habits, that give us the strength to do what is right and live holy lives. The four moral virtues are also called cardinal virtues. The word *cardinal* comes from a word meaning "to hinge on." The four cardinal virtues are:

Prudence. Prudence helps us evaluate situations and judge whether they will lead us to do good or evil.

Justice. Justice directs us to give to God what rightfully belongs to him and to give to our neighbors what rightfully belongs to them.

Fortitude. Fortitude keeps us steady in doing what is good, especially when difficulties arise.

Temperance. Temperance helps us use and enjoy things in a way that is not harmful to us or others.

Our moral life and moral decision making hinge on the moral virtues. They help us live as children of God and followers of Christ.

Read this situation. Name a moral virtue that will help Robert make and put into practice a good decision.

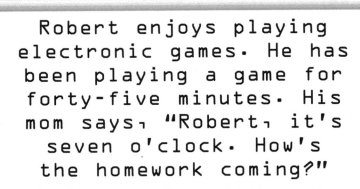

Robert enjoys playing electronic games. He has been playing a game for forty-five minutes. His mom says, "Robert, it's seven o'clock. How's the homework coming?"

Our Church Makes a Difference

Examination of Conscience

Christians have always set aside time to think about their decisions. We call this practice an examination of conscience. Each day we examine our conscience, usually at bedtime. Examining our conscience helps us build up our relationship with God and others.

Making a Retreat

The word *retreat* has many meanings. One meaning is "a quiet place." Catholics often set aside time to go to a quiet place. While they are there, they think and pray about the way they are living their faith. Sometimes Catholics go away to a retreat house. They stay there for a day, overnight, a few days, a week, or longer.

Retreat houses organize retreats for adult women, for adult men, for married couples, and for singles.

They also hold retreats for youth groups and young people preparing for Confirmation. Catholics make a retreat so they take time to grow in their relationship with God and plan ways to live holy lives.

Talk about some of the ways your parish helps you spend time growing in your love for God and for others.

What Difference Does Faith Make in My Life?

Each day you try to grow as a Christian and make decisions to live the life that God asks you to live.

You are the commentator of a student talk show, "Decisions! Decisions!" Today the topic is "Helpful Decisions Made by Fifth Graders." Create a dialogue you might have with a student about making good decisions and the good consequences that come from those decisions.

Decisions! Decisions!

_____

_____

_____

_____

_____

_____

_____

_____

_____

My Faith Choice

This week I will try to be more aware of how I go about making good decisions. Before I make an important decision I will

_____

_____ .

An Examination of Conscience

An examination of conscience is like a mini-retreat. Set aside time each day. Use this examination of conscience.

1. Sit in a comfortable place. Remember that God is with you.
2. Spend some time thinking about the day.
3. Answer these questions:
   a. How have I shown or not shown love and respect for God?
   b. How have I shown or not shown love and respect for myself?
   c. How have I shown or not shown love and respect for other people?
   d. How have I used or misused the gift of God's creation?
4. Spend some time talking to God. Ask him to help you make better decisions.
5. Promise that you will try to do your best.

We Remember

Fill in the circle next to each correct answer.

1. A _____ is a habit or spiritual power that helps us do what is right and avoid what is wrong.

   ○ temptation   ○ conscience   ○ virtue

2. Our _____ is our ability to know God, our self, and other people more and more.

   ○ intellect   ○ free will   ○ soul

3. A _____ is the gift of God that is part of every person and helps us know and judge what is right and wrong.

   ○ virtue   ○ free will   ○ conscience

4. _____ is the cardinal virtue that keeps us steady when problems arise in living holy lives.

   ○ justice   ○ fortitude   ○ kindness

To Help You Remember

1. Moral decisions help us grow as children of God and live as followers of Jesus Christ.

2. Conscience is our ability to know and judge what is right and what is wrong.

3. The cardinal virtues of prudence, justice, fortitude, and temperance are good habits that help us live holy lives.

This Week . . .

In chapter 18, "Making Christian Decisions," your child learned about the importance of making moral decisions. Such decisions guide us in living as children of God and followers of Christ. Each of us has been given a conscience, an intellect, a free will, and feelings, or emotions. All these natural gifts give us the ability to make decisions that guide us in living holy lives. Throughout our entire life we cooperate with the grace of the Holy Spirit and work at forming a good conscience and developing virtues. The four virtues of prudence, justice, fortitude, and temperance are called the cardinal virtues. These virtues strengthen our desire and ability to choose what is good, to overcome the temptation to do evil, and avoid doing what is not good.

For more on the teachings of the Catholic Church on conscience, cardinal virtues, and making moral decisions, see *Catechism of the Catholic Church* paragraph numbers 1699–1709, 1716–1724, 1730–1742, 1762–1770, 1776–1794, and 1803–1811.

Sharing God's Word

Read together Wisdom 8:7. Emphasize that the four cardinal virtues play a pivotal role in helping us make good decisions to live holy lives.

Praying

In this chapter your child learned one form of an examination of conscience. Use this examination of conscience. Follow the steps on page 163.

Making a Difference

Choose one of the following activities to do as a family or design a similar activity of your own.

- Invite family members to share the things that help them develop a good conscience. Encourage each other to make decisions to live holy lives.

- An examination of conscience helps us reflect on our moral decisions. Talk about why it is important to think about our moral decisions before, during, and after we make them.

- Identify ways your family can help one another make decisions to live a holy life. Choose one thing you will do this week to help each other.

For more ideas on ways your family can live your faith, visit the "Faith First for Families" page at **www.FaithFirst.com**. Click on "Make a Difference" for ideas on how your family can share God's love with others this week.

The Beatitudes
A Scripture Story

We Pray

Bless the LORD, my soul;
all my being, bless his
holy name!

PSALM 103:1

Father, send the
Holy Spirit to guide us
to live as faithful
members of your
holy people.   Amen.

*Where do you think true
happiness comes from?*

Everyone wants to be
happy. Everyone spends
their whole life seeking
happiness. Jesus taught
the Beatitudes to help us
learn the true meaning of
happiness.

What are the Beatitudes?

Saint Elizabeth Ann Seton,
stained glass

165

Bible Background

Faith Focus

How do the Beatitudes help us make decisions to live as Christians?

Faith Vocabulary

Sermon on the Mount. The teachings of Jesus that are grouped together in chapters 5, 6, and 7 of the Gospel of Matthew.

Beatitudes. The sayings or teachings of Jesus that are found in the Sermon on the Mount that describe both the qualities and the actions of people blessed by God.

The Sermon on the Mount

During his life on earth, Jesus taught his disciples many things. He gave his disciples concrete guidelines on how he wanted them to live. Matthew has gathered many of the teachings of Jesus in chapters 5, 6, and 7 of his Gospel. This part of Matthew's Gospel is called the **Sermon on the Mount.**

The Sermon on the Mount begins with the **Beatitudes.** The Beatitudes are the sayings or teachings of Jesus that describe both the qualities and the actions of people blessed by God.

The words *blessed* and *kingdom* are the key to understanding Jesus' teachings in the Beatitudes.

Blessed. The Jewish people described people who

Participants signing up for Walk for Hunger, Walk for Hunger Wall, Boston, Massachusetts

trusted and hoped in God above everyone and everything else as "blessed."

Kingdom. The Jewish people living in Jesus' time were under the rule of the Romans. They wanted to be free of that rule and prayed that God would establish the kingdom he had promised to Abraham, Moses, and David. Jesus' listeners and disciples hoped that Jesus would bring about that kingdom.

Describe some of the ways you seek happiness. Are these ways that God would call "blessed"?

Reading the Word of God

The Beatitudes

Jesus traveled throughout Galilee and Judea preaching the good news of the coming of the kingdom of God. One day a crowd followed Jesus up a mountainside in Galilee. Seeing the crowd, he began to teach them. He said:

"Blessed are the poor in
spirit,
for theirs is the
kingdom of heaven.
Blessed are they who
mourn,
for they will be
comforted.
Blessed are the meek,
for they will inherit
the land.
Blessed are they who
hunger and thirst
for righteousness,
for they will be
satisfied.
Blessed are the merciful,
for they will be
shown mercy.
Blessed are the clean
of heart,
for they will see God.
Blessed are the
peacemakers,
for they will be called
children of God.
Blessed are they who
are persecuted for
the sake of
righteousness,

for theirs is the
kingdom of
heaven."
MATTHEW 5:3–12

Jesus concluded by telling his listeners that living the Beatitudes would not be easy. People would make fun of them and even persecute them. He told them to have the courage to live the Beatitudes. If they did, they would discover happiness. He said, "Rejoice and be glad, for your reward will be great in heaven."

Describe a person you know or have learned about who lives the Beatitudes.

The Blessed

What Jesus' listeners did not yet understand was that the kingdom of God, or the happiness that Jesus was speaking about, was not a kingdom of power on earth. It was a different kind of kingdom. By understanding the meaning of each of the Beatitudes, we can better understand Jesus' teachings on what it means to be truly blessed by God.

The poor in spirit. People who are poor in spirit place all their trust in God.

Those who mourn. People who mourn have suffered a loss in their lives. They are strong because they know God is always with them.

The meek. People who are meek are considerate. They treat others kindly and respectfully.

Those who hunger and thirst for righteousness. These people work so that everyone is treated fairly and justly.

The merciful. Merciful people are generous and kind to others.

The clean of heart. The clean of heart place God above everyone and everything else in their lives.

The peacemakers. Peacemakers work to solve problems without harming anyone and to build the kind of world God wants.

Those persecuted for righteousness. People who work for righteousness do what God wants, even when it is very difficult to do so.

The Beatitudes are guides for living as Jesus taught us to live. All our actions show that we live for the kingdom Jesus announced was "at hand." The rewards promised to the blessed will be received in the kingdom of God.

The headline "Workers Meet to Settle Salary Demands" might describe the Beatitude "Blessed are the peacemakers." Create a headline for one other Beatitude.

Beatitudes in Action

_____

_____

_____

_____

Habitat for Humanity

Habitat for Humanity International is a Christian housing organization. It brings together Catholic and other Christian volunteers to work together for justice and righteousness. They build "simple, decent, and affordable housing in partnership with those in need of adequate housing."

Habitat for Humanity volunteers have built more than 150,000 homes all over the world. This includes more than 50,000 in the United States. These homes are for people who cannot afford to buy a home of their own.

Habitat for Humanity volunteers build homes for people of all races, religions, and ethnic groups.

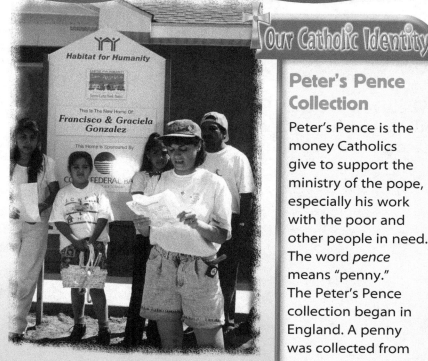

Their work is a sign of God's love for all people and helps all people place their trust in him. You can imagine the happiness that families feel when they move into a home built by Habitat for Humanity.

How does your parish help to build a better world by living the Beatitudes?

What Difference Does Faith Make in My Life?

When you live the Beatitudes, you are a sign to others of what it means to be blessed by God. You have your eyes on living in the kingdom of heaven.

Each of these actions is one way of living a Beatitude. Think about the two actions described below. Then name the Beatitude it puts into action and write one way you have lived that Beatitude.

Living the Beatitudes

Action	Beatitude	How I Lived It
1. You are kind to someone others are picking on.	_____ _____ _____ _____	_____ _____ _____ _____
2. You listen to someone you disagree with. Together you solve your problem.	_____ _____ _____ _____	_____ _____ _____ _____

My Faith Choice

I believe that the Holy Spirit calls me to live the Beatitudes. This week I will

_____

_____.

Prayer to Live the Beatitudes

In a prayer of petition, we ask God to help us live for the kingdom of God. Pray this prayer of petition. Ask God to help you live the Beatitudes.

Leader: Loving Father, send us the Holy Spirit.
Teach us to be poor in spirit

All: **that we will receive the gift of the kingdom of heaven.**

Leader: Teach us to mourn

All: **that we will receive the gift of your comfort.**

Leader: Teach us to be meek

All: **that we will inherit the earth.**

Leader: Teach us to hunger and thirst for righteousness

All: **that we will be satisfied.**

Leader: Teach us to be merciful

All: **that we will be shown mercy.**

Leader: Teach us to be clean of heart

All: **that we will see you.**

Leader: Teach us to be peacemakers

All: **that we will be called children of God.**

Leader: Teach us to have courage when we are treated harmfully because of our love for you

All: **that we will receive the gift of the kingdom of heaven.**

BASED ON MATTHEW 5:3–10

We Remember

Match the parts of the Beatitudes.

___ 1. "Blessed are the meek

___ 2. "Blessed are the peacemakers

___ 3. "Blessed are the poor in spirit

___ 4. "Blessed are the clean of heart

___ 5. "Blessed are they who mourn

a. for theirs is the kingdom of heaven."

b. for they will see God."

c. for they will be comforted."

d. for they will inherit the land."

e. for they will be called children of God."

To Help You Remember

1. The Beatitudes show ways Jesus wants his disciples to live.

2. The Beatitudes are sayings of Jesus that describe the qualities and actions of people blessed by God.

3. The Beatitudes guide us to prepare the way for the coming of the kingdom of God, which will come about at the end of time.

This Week . . .

In chapter 19, "The Beatitudes: A Scripture Story," your child learned about the Beatitudes that are found in the Sermon on the Mount in Matthew's Gospel. The Beatitudes name qualities and rewards of those blessed by God. The disciples of Jesus are called to live in such a way that we witness to the coming of the kingdom of heaven. We are to be living signs of the blessedness, or happiness, God wishes for all.

For more on the teachings of the Catholic Church on the human vocation to beatitude, or happiness, see *Catechism of the Catholic Church* paragraph numbers 1716–1724.

Sharing God's Word

Read together Matthew 5:3–12. Emphasize that Jesus taught the Beatitudes to identify people who were truly blessed by God.

Praying

In this chapter your child prayed a prayer of petition, asking God for the grace to live the Beatitudes. Read and pray together this prayer on page 171.

Making a Difference

Choose one of the following activities to do as a family or design a similar activity of your own.

- We live the Beatitudes when we are peacemakers. Name ways that you can live as peacemakers at home, at school, at work, and in your community.

- Write each of the Beatitudes on an index card and put the cards in a container near the entrance of your home. Each day this week have each family member choose a card, read it, place it back in the container, and try to put the Beatitude on it into practice that day.

- In the Sermon on the Mount, Jesus taught that happiness comes from living as God created us to live. Talk about why living as a child of God is the only way to find true happiness.

For more ideas on ways your family can live your faith, visit the "Faith First for Families" page at **www.FaithFirst.com**. Click on "Contemporary Issues" to find an article on an especially interesting topic.

Live as Children of Light

We Pray

The LORD is my light and my salvation.

PSALM 27:1

God, our loving Father, fill our hearts with light and lead us to your Son. Amen.

What makes every person special?

God created us to be holy. When you think of a holy person, who do you think of? We live holy lives when we live our Catholic faith.

What are the qualities of a holy person?

Our Call to Holiness

Faith Vocabulary

sanctifying grace. The gift of God's life and love that makes us holy and helps us live holy lives.

actual grace. The gift of God's presence with us to help us live as children of God and followers of Jesus Christ.

Jesus, Our Model of Holiness

God created every person to be holy. God created us in his image and likeness. The Scriptures tell us:

"Be holy because I [am] holy." 1 PETER 1:16

Holiness is sharing in the very life and love of God. Jesus lived and taught the way of holiness. After he taught his disciples the Beatitudes, Jesus told his disciples they were to be lights in the world (see Matthew 5:14–16). At the Last Supper he told them how to do this. He said:

"As the Father loves me, so I also love you. . . . This I command you: love one another." JOHN 15:9, 17

Our choices—our words and actions—are to show our love for God and for one another. Each day we ask the Holy Spirit to help us try our best to love, forgive, and care for others as Jesus showed us.

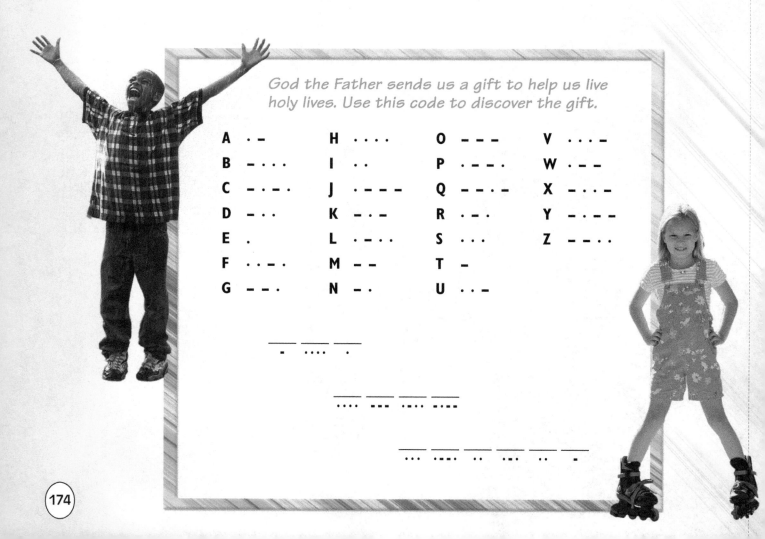

God the Father sends us a gift to help us live holy lives. Use this code to discover the gift.

A · −	H · · · ·	O − − −	V · · · −
B − · · ·	I · ·	P · − − ·	W · − −
C − · − ·	J · − − −	Q − − · −	X − · · −
D − · ·	K − · −	R · − ·	Y − · − −
E ·	L · − · ·	S · · ·	Z − − · ·
F · · − ·	M − −	T −	
G − − ·	N − ·	U · · −	

− · · · · ·

· · · · − − − · · · · · · · · ·

− − − − − −
· · · · · · · · · · · · · · −

Perpetua and Felicity

Saint Perpetua and Saint Felicity are examples of the power of God's grace working in our lives. These North African women suffered martyrdom because of their faithfulness to Christ. They gave each other the kiss of peace as they were attacked by wild animals. The Church celebrates the feast day of Saints Perpetua and Felicity on March 7.

Living by God's Grace

Our parents share the gift of life and their love and their faith in Jesus with us. Through Baptism, God shares the gift of his life and love with us. We call this gift **sanctifying grace**. The word *sanctifying* means "making holy." Through this grace all that separates us from God is taken away. Sin is forgiven. We are made holy.

God also gives us the gift of his help to live holy lives. We call this help from God **actual grace**. The Holy Spirit teaches us and helps us live as followers of Jesus Christ. Without the grace of the Holy Spirit, we could never live as children of God.

We strengthen our love for God and receive his grace to live holy lives when we take part in the celebration of the sacraments, especially the Eucharist. Reading the Bible and praying also help us say yes to God's invitation to live as his children.

What might you do that shows you are saying yes to God's gift of grace?

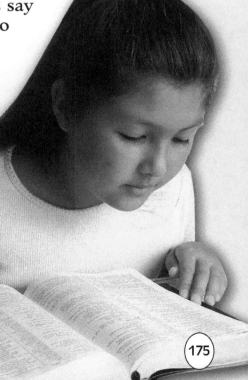

Choosing the Way of Holiness

We can choose to live Jesus' command, "Love one another," or we can choose not to live it. We can choose to make decisions not to live the way of holiness. When we freely choose not to live as God wants us to live, we sin. The decision to sin can begin with a temptation. All sin offends God and hurts us. All sins are not the same.

Mortal sin. Serious, or grave, sins that separate us from God are called mortal sins. Three things are necessary to commit a mortal sin They are:

1. The thing that we choose to do or not to do must be very seriously wrong.
2. We must know that what we are choosing to do or not to do is seriously wrong.
3. We must freely choose to do what we know is seriously wrong.

Venial sins. Less serious sins are called venial sins. A sin is a venial sin when one, two, or three of the things named above for a mortal sin are missing. Venial sins damage and weaken our love for God and for others. They do not break our relationship with God. Ignoring our venial sins or failing to be sorry for them can lead us to sin seriously.

Keeping our eyes focused on God and trying our best to live a holy life is the best way to make moral decisions. It is the best way to say yes to God in big things and in little things.

Take a moment. Pray to the Holy Spirit. Ask the Holy Spirit to help you say yes to God and no to sin.

Venerable Father Solanus, top left, in Detroit Soup Kitchen

Venerable Father Casey

God invites everyone to share his life and love. He invites everyone to live a holy life. Sometimes people who live holy lives are named saints, or canonized, by the Church. The Church has named Bernard Casey a Venerable of the Church. This is the first step in naming him a saint of the Church.

Bernard Casey was the sixth child of a family of ten boys and six girls. They lived on a farm in Wisconsin near the Mississippi River. At the age of twenty-one he entered St. Francis Seminary in Milwaukee. Five years later he received the name Solanus when he entered the Franciscan Capuchin Order.

After he was ordained a priest, Father Solanus devoted his life to serving the sick and the poor in many places in the United States. In 1929 during the Depression when most families were hungry and without money, he worked with his brother Franciscans to set up the Detroit Soup Kitchen. The work of this soup kitchen still continues today.

Father Solanus Casey truly loved others as Jesus loved him. One day before he died, he said, "I looked on my whole life as giving, and I want to give until there is nothing left."

Our Catholic Identity

Canonization

When the Church names a person a saint, it declares that the person has lived a holy life and is now in heaven. The process the Church uses to do this is called canonization.

Think of a person you know who is living a holy life. How is that person making a difference in the lives of other people?

Venerable Father Solanus, top left, passing out bread

What Difference Does Faith Make in My Life?

You are holy and are called to live a holy life.

Faced with these situations, what are some good choices that would help you grow in holiness?

Growing in Holiness

A friend of yours makes the team but you do not.
How might you react?

I would _____

_____

_____ .

Your parents really want you to go someplace important
with the family, but you want to go somewhere with your friends.
How would you feel? What would you do?

I would feel _____

_____ .

I would _____

_____

_____ .

My Faith Choice

This week I will look for ways to make choices
that will help me grow in holiness. I will

_____

_____ .

We Pray

Praying a Psalm

The Church prays the Psalms every day. Pray these Psalm verses. Ask God to help you walk the way of holiness that Jesus taught.

Group 1: Make known to me your ways, LORD; teach me your paths.

Group 2: Guide me in your truth and teach me, for you are God my savior.

Group 1: For you I wait all the long day, because of your goodness, LORD.

Group 2: Let honesty and virtue preserve me; I wait for you, O LORD.

PSALM 25:4–5, 21

We Remember

Solve this crossword puzzle.

To Help You Remember

1. When we live as images of God, we live holy lives.

2. When we sin, we choose not to live holy lives.

3. The grace of God helps us live holy lives.

DOWN

1. Serious sin by which we choose to separate ourselves from God's love

2. Grace that is the gift of God's life and love that makes us holy

ACROSS

3. Sins that weaken our love for God and for others

4. Grace that helps us live as children of God and followers of Jesus

5. Living as children of God

Crossword answer: 5. d i s c i p l e

This Week . . .

In chapter 20, "Live as Children of Light," your child learned more about the call of every person to live a holy life. Christians are called to live the way of holiness Jesus lived and taught his disciples to live. Through Baptism we receive the gift of sanctifying grace, the gift of holiness. We are made sharers in the life and love of God the Father, the Son, and the Holy Spirit. We are joined to Christ and receive the gift of the Holy Spirit and the graces to live as children of God. God gave us the gift of freedom. When we freely choose not to live as we know God wants us to live, we sin. We can accept or reject God's invitation and his help to live a holy life.

For more on the teachings of the Catholic Church on sin and grace, see *Catechism of the Catholic Church* paragraph numbers 1846–1869 and 1987–2016.

Sharing God's Word

Read together 1 Peter 1:15–16. Emphasize that God created every person to be holy.

Praying

In this chapter your child prayed a prayer based on Psalm 25. Read and pray together this prayer on page 179.

Making a Difference

Choose one of the following activities to do as a family or design a similar activity of your own.

- Cooperating with God's grace helps us grow in holiness. Name some people who help you make choices to live a holy life.

- Ask each family member to think of a person they believe lives a holy life. Then have family members share how those people are making a difference in the lives of others.

- Ask each family member to share the name of their favorite saint. Together research the lives of your family's favorite saints on the *Catholic Encyclopedia* Web site. Talk about why that person was named a saint, a model of holiness.

For more ideas on ways your family can live your faith, visit the "Faith First for Families" page at **www.FaithFirst.com**. Click on "Family Prayer." Plan to pray this prayer together this week.

God Is Love
A Scripture Story

21

We Pray

Give thanks to the LORD,
 who is good,
 whose love endures
 forever.

PSALM 118:1

Father of all goodness,
may we live our life
in Christ, your Son,
with joy and express it
in love.   Amen.

What are some ways you share your thoughts and feelings?

We share our thoughts and feelings with one another in many ways. God speaks to us about himself in the Bible. The First Letter of John in the New Testament tells us, "God is love" (1 John 4:16).

Why do you think God wants us to know this about him?

Bible Background

Faith Focus

How does reading the First Letter of John help us understand what it means to love God?

Faith Vocabulary

catholic letters.
The seven New Testament letters that bear the names of the Apostles John, Peter, Jude, and James.

The Catholic Letters

Prayerfully reading the Scriptures with other people or alone helps us come to know and love God. The Church has named the forty-six books of the Old Testament and the twenty-seven books of the New Testament as the inspired word of God.

The New Testament

- The four accounts of the Gospel
- The Acts of the Apostles
- The thirteen letters, or epistles, of Paul the Apostle
- The seven catholic letters
- The Letter to the Hebrews
- The Book of Revelation

The seven catholic letters were written to all Christians. The word *catholic* means "universal" or "for everyone."

The Catholic Letters

- Letter of James
- First Letter of Peter
- Second Letter of Peter
- First Letter of John
- Second Letter of John
- Third Letter of John
- Letter of Jude

Each of these seven letters has the name of an Apostle in its title. This tells us that the Church believes that these letters pass on to Christians the authentic teachings of the Apostles.

Share your beliefs about Jesus in an e-mail to a friend. Describe your thoughts and feelings here.

Send:

To:

Subject:

Reading the Word of God

God Is Love

Three of the seven catholic letters are attributed to Saint John the Apostle. This means that they share his teachings with us. The First Letter of John helps us understand the depth of God's love for us. In this letter we read:

Beloved, let us love one another, because love is of God; everyone who loves is begotten by God and knows God. Whoever is without love does not know God, for God is love. . . . God is love, and whoever remains in love remains in God and God in him. . . . If anyone says, "I love God," but hates his brother, he is a liar; for whoever does not love a brother whom he has seen cannot love God whom he has not seen. This is the commandment we have from him: whoever loves God must also love his brother.

1 JOHN 4:7–8, 16, 20–21

As we read this letter, God tells us about himself, "God is love." He also tells us about ourselves, "Whoever loves God must also love his brother." We are to love one another if we really want to live in God's love.

What difference would it make for the world if everyone really understood and lived the message about God and about ourselves in the First Letter of John?

183

Love of God and Others

The First Letter of John teaches what Christian love means. The letter goes back to where all love begins—in God. John says, "[L]ove is of God" and "God is love."

God gives us a special gift to give us the power to love him. It is the gift of the theological virtue of love. The virtue of love gives us the power to return to God the love he shares with us. It gives us the power to make God's love the most important thing in our lives.

We know that God's love is taking hold of us by the way we treat others. John tells us we are called to love others as God loves us. We care for each other in ways that are real and not just in words. In giving us his Son, God the Father gave us the generous gift of his love. If we are to imitate this generous gift of divine love, we do not ask "What's in it for me?" before we help someone. Once we realize how much God loves us, we can begin to love others as he loves them.

Write about one sign of God's love you experienced this week.

Showing God's Love

Our Church Makes a Difference

Witnesses for Christ

From the first days of the Church, Christians have lived as Christ and given their lives out of love for God and people. Here are but a few of the thousands of Christian martyrs who have willingly risked and given up their lives as they proclaimed the good news of God's love for all people:

- Ursuline Sister Dorothy Kazel, Maryknoll Sisters Ita Ford and Maura Clarke, and lay missionary Jean Donovan were shot and killed for working with the poor and preaching the Gospel in El Salvador in Central America in 1980.

- Sister Aloysius Maria, a Missionary of Charity, was killed by rebels in Sierra Leone in 1999.

- Father Albino Saluhakku, a priest of the diocese of Huambo in Angola, and two catechists working with him were killed in 1999.

- Bishop Benjamin de Jesus, a member of the Oblates of Mary Immaculate, was gunned down in 1998 outside the cathedral in Jolo in the Philippines.

- Marist Brothers Servando Mayor Garcia, Miguel Angel Isla Lucio, Fernando de la Fuente, and Julio Rodriguez Jorge were murdered in 1995 in Eastern Zaire by Rwandan militants while working with Rwandan refugees.

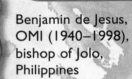

Our Catholic Identity

Christian Martyrs

The word *martyr* means "witness." Christian martyrs are witnesses for Christ. They make the greatest sacrifice of all to live the Great Commandment. Because of their love for God and people they freely choose to suffer death rather than stop loving God and their neighbors.

Benjamin de Jesus, OMI (1940–1998), bishop of Jolo, Philippines

Sister Maura Clarke, MM (1931–1980)

Who do you know who is suffering in your community? How can you work with others to help them?

185

What Difference Does Faith Make in My Life?

Each day your deeds and words show your love for God.

Create a picture story of your actions speaking loudly about God's love.

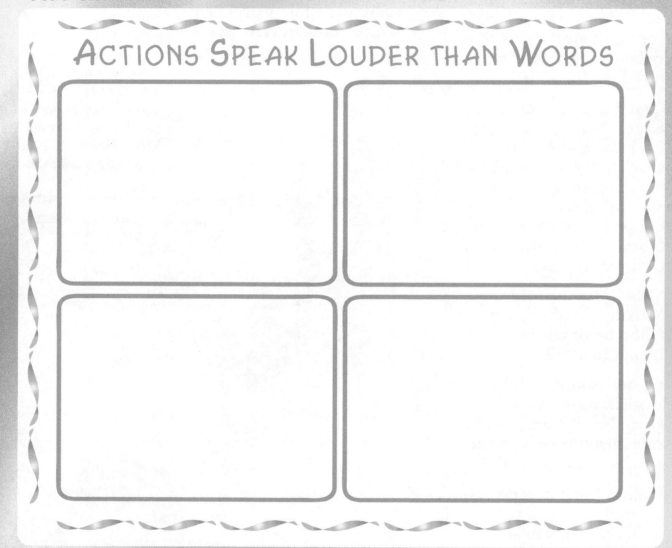

ACTIONS SPEAK LOUDER THAN WORDS

My Faith Choice

This week I will show that I love God.
I will

_____

_____.

We Pray

An Act of Love

God created us to share in his love and to share that love with others. Jesus reminded us of this when he taught about the Great Commandment. He most clearly revealed this when he freely gave his life on the cross. Pray this act of love alone and with other people.

O my God, I love you above all things,

with my whole heart and soul,

because you are all good and worthy of all my love.

I love my neighbor as myself for the love of you.

I forgive all who have injured me,

and I ask pardon of all whom I have injured.

Amen.

We Remember

Circle the word or phrase that completes each sentence correctly.

1. There are _____ catholic letters.
   a. **two**   b. **five**   c. **seven**

2. The catholic letters are part of the _____.
   a. **New Testament**   b. **Old Testament**
   c. *Catechism of the Catholic Church*

3. The catholic letters each have the name of an _____.
   a. **Evangelist**   b. **Apostle**   c. **pope**

4. The catholic letters are addressed to _____ Christians.
   a. **all**   b. **some**   c. **no**

5. The First Letter of _____ tells us that a person cannot love God and hate other people.
   a. **John**   b. **Paul**   c. **Matthew**

To Help You Remember

1. The seven catholic letters in the New Testament were written to all Christians.

2. The First Letter of John reveals to us that "God is love."

3. If we truly love God, we love others as God loves them.

This Week . . .

In chapter 21, "God Is Love: A Scripture Story," your child learned about the catholic letters in the New Testament, in particular the First Letter of John. The First Letter of John reveals that "God is love" (1 John 4:8). As children of God, who is love, we are to love others. If we say we love God and do not love others, we are liars.

For more on the teachings of the Catholic Church on the attributes, or qualities, of God that he has revealed about himself, see *Catechism of the Catholic Church* paragraph numbers 199–221.

Sharing God's Word

Read together 1 John 4:7–21. Emphasize that in this passage John teaches "God is love, and whoever remains in love remains in God and God in him."

Praying

In this chapter your child learned to pray an act of love. Read and pray together this prayer on page 187.

Making a Difference

Choose one of the following activities to do as a family or design a similar activity of your own.

- Make a banner with the words "Whoever loves God must also love his brothers and sisters." Decorate the banner and hang it in your home where it can remind everyone of the importance of loving one another.

- We show our love for God by loving others. Research the ways your parish shows its love for God by loving others.

- Talk about how your family puts your love for God into action. Choose one thing you can do this week to put your love for God into action as a family.

For more ideas on ways your family can live your faith, visit the "Faith First for Families" page at **www.FaithFirst.com**. Check out "Bible Stories." Read and discuss the Bible story this week.

Living Our Covenant with God

22

We Pray

LORD, teach me the way
    of your laws. . . .
Give me insight to
    observe your
    teaching,
to keep it with all
    my heart.
                    PSALM 119:33–34

Father, blessed be your Son, Jesus, whom you sent to show us how we can love you. Amen.

Which of the Ten Commandments can you name?

Rules help us respect one another and live together as a community. The Ten Commandments outline our responsibilities to love and respect God, others, and ourselves.

Why is it important for all people to obey the Ten Commandments?

Moses carrying stone tablets containing the Ten Commandments, stained glass

189

Living as the People of God

How do the First, Second, and Third Commandments tell us to live?

Faith Vocabulary

Ten Commandments. The laws of the Covenant revealed to Moses and the Israelites on Mount Sinai.

Covenant. The solemn agreement that God entered into with people, promising that he would be their God and they were to be his chosen people.

Rock formations on Mount Sinai

Living the Covenant

The story of God's revelation of the **Ten Commandments** is part of the story of the **Covenant.** After Moses led the Israelites out of slavery in Egypt, they journeyed for forty years in the desert. During this time, the Israelites grew angry with God, with Moses, and with one another. They forgot the Covenant God had made with them.

Sacred Scripture tells us that God saw all that was happening and called Moses up to the mountain. There he gave Moses the Ten Commandments to guide his people in living the Covenant. After Moses came down from the mountain, he explained to the Israelites:

"These then are the commandments, . . . which the LORD, your God, has ordered that you be taught to observe."

DEUTERONOMY 6:1

Jesus fulfilled these laws revealed to Moses by God. They guide the followers of Christ in living the New Covenant that God has made with all people.

Imagine you are Moses. What would you tell the people when you came down from the mountain?

_____

_____

_____

_____

_____

_____

_____

190

The First Three Commandments

The First, Second, and Third Commandments describe our privilege and responsibility to worship God. Everyone should be free to worship God according to their conscience.

The First Commandment.

I am the LORD your God: you shall not have strange gods before me.
BASED ON EXODUS 20:2–3

Through the First Commandment, God calls us to believe and hope in him and love him above all else. We are not to let things, such as money or being popular, become more important to us than God.

The Second Commandment.

You shall not take the name of the LORD, your God, in vain. EXODUS 20:7

The Second Commandment teaches us to use God's name truthfully. We use God's name in vain when we take an oath to tell the truth and lie. When we do this, we call upon God as a witness to a lie as if it were the truth. We also use God's name in vain when we curse or swear or use the name *God* or *Jesus* in anger, or in any inappropriate way.

Choose the First or Second Commandment. Describe what might happen when people faithfully live that Commandment.

New American citizens swearing loyalty at a naturalization ceremony

Sunday is the Lord's Day for Christians. It is the day on which Jesus was raised from the dead. Taking part in Mass on the Lord's Day, either on Saturday evening or Sunday, is a serious responsibility for Catholics. Catholics who do not have a serious reason for not participating in Mass, such as an illness, and deliberately choose not to fulfill this responsibility commit a serious sin.

The Lord's Day is a time to worship God the Creator. It is a time to rest from our work and make sure all the work we do is God's work. It is a time to nourish our faith and our life.

What are some of the ways you keep Sunday, the Lord's Day, holy?

_____

_____

_____

_____

_____

_____

_____

_____

_____

The Third Commandment.
Remember to keep holy the LORD's Day.
BASED ON EXODUS 20:8

In the story of creation in the Bible, we read that "God blessed the seventh day and made it holy, because on it he rested from all the work he had done in creation" (Genesis 2:3). For the Israelites and the Jewish people today, the seventh day of the week is a holy day and the Sabbath.

Our Church Makes a Difference

Holy Days of Obligation

Catholics around the world set aside the Lord's Day to give public witness to God and his loving plan of salvation. They also gather and celebrate God's love on holy days of obligation. All Catholics have the responsibility to celebrate these days by taking part in the celebration of the Eucharist.

Fishermen carry statue of Madonna of Portosalvo to celebrate the feast of the Assumption, Ragusa, Sicily, Italy

In some places these days are celebrated with processions and festivals. Special costumes are worn and statues are carried through the streets. Sometimes there is singing and dancing. These celebrations remind Catholics and all who witness them that God is the Father of all people. He invites everyone to respond to his love with faith and trust.

How does celebrating holy days of obligation invite all people to grow in their love for God?

Candles illuminating a cemetery, All Saints' Day, Lacombe, Louisiana

Christmas, Bethlehem, Israel

193

What Difference Does Faith Make in My Life?

You are growing in your love for God each day. Many things you do show others that God is at the center of your life.

In each part of the circle write one thing you can do to help you make God the center of your life.

The Center of My Life

GOD

My Faith Choice

This week I will keep Sunday as a holy and special day dedicated to the Lord. I will

_____

_____ .

You Are God

The Te Deum ("You Are God") is an ancient hymn of the Church. Written in the 300s, this is a great hymn of praise of God.

All: **You are God: we praise you.**

Group 1: You are God: we praise you;
you are God: we acclaim you;

Group 2: you are the eternal Father:
all creation worships you.

All: **You are God: we praise you.**

All: **You are God: we praise you.**

Group 1: The glorious company of apostles praises you.
The noble fellowship of prophets praises you.
The white-robed army of martyrs praises you.

Group 2: Throughout the world the holy Church acclaims you:
Father, of majesty unbounded,
your true and only Son, worthy of all worship,
and the Holy Spirit, advocate and guide.

All: **You are God: we praise you.**

Peter Paul Matthew

Isaiah Ezekiel Jeremiah

Agnes   Stephen   Cecilia

We Remember

Match the terms in column A with their descriptions in column B.

Column A

_____ 1. First Commandment

_____ 2. Second Commandment

_____ 3. Third Commandment

Column B

a. Keep the Lord's Day as a holy day.

b. Use God's name truthfully and respectfully.

c. Worship only God and love him above all things.

To Help You Remember

1. God revealed the Ten Commandments to guide us in making moral decisions.

2. The First, Second, and Third Commandments describe our privilege and responsibility to worship God.

3. The Lord's Day is a holy day and a time to rest from our work. Sunday is the Lord's Day for Christians.

This Week . . .

In chapter 22, "Living Our Covenant with God," your child learned more about the Ten Commandments. The Ten Commandments guide us in living the Covenant that binds God and humankind. The First, Second, and Third Commandments describe our privilege and responsibility to worship, respect, and reverence God as God. The First Commandment calls us to believe in, hope in, and love God above all else. The Second Commandment teaches the fundamental human responsibility to respect God by only calling on his name truthfully to witness to what we do and say. The Third Commandment obliges us to worship God together at Mass and to nourish our relationship with both him and our family.

For more on the teachings of the Catholic Church on the First, Second, and Third Commandments, see *Catechism of the Catholic Church* paragraph numbers 2083–2132, 2142–2159, and 2168–2188.

Sharing God's Word

Read together Exodus 19:1–20 and 20:1–17. Emphasize that God gave Moses the Ten Commandments to guide his people in making decisions to live the Covenant.

Praying

In this chapter your child learned to pray the Te Deum. Read and pray together this prayer on page 195.

Making a Difference

Choose one of the following activities to do as a family or design a similar activity of your own.

- The First, Second, and Third Commandments teach us to show our love and respect for God. Talk about how you show your love and respect for God during Mass, and how you show your love and respect for God at home.

- The Third Commandment teaches us to keep holy the Lord's Day, Sunday. How does this Commandment help us grow in faith? How does this Commandment help our parish grow in faith?

- Talk about how your family makes Sunday a special and holy day. Choose one thing you can do this week to make Sunday a day for the Lord.

For more ideas on ways your family can live your faith, visit the "Faith First for Families" page at **www.FaithFirst.com**. Click on "Games" and make learning fun for your child.

Love Your Neighbor as Yourself

23

We Pray

Make known to me
your ways, LORD;
teach me your paths.
PSALM 25:4

O God, we love you
above all things,
because you are
all-good and worthy
of all love. We love our
neighbor as ourselves
for the love of you.
Amen.

*What are some of the ways
we show respect for one
another?*

We show our respect for
people by the way we
treat them. Jesus taught
that we show our respect
for God and for people
by living the Great
Commandment. The
Ten Commandments
help us live the Great
Commandment.

*Which of the Ten
Commandments teach us
to love and respect one
another?*

197

Respecting Ourselves and Others

Faith Focus

What do the Ten Commandments teach us about loving our neighbor as we love ourselves?

Faith Vocabulary

chastity. The virtue that is the good habit of respecting and honoring our sexuality that guides us to share our love with others in appropriate ways.

justice. The moral, or cardinal, virtue that is the good habit of giving God and all people what is rightfully due to them.

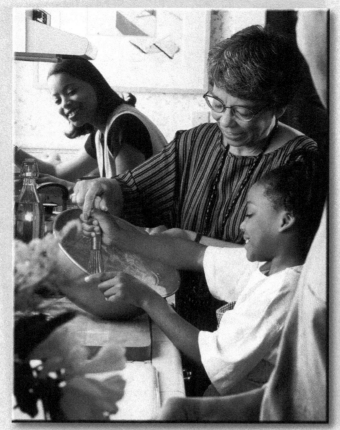

The Fourth Through the Tenth Commandments

Jesus taught that there is one Great Commandment, which has two parts. We are to love God, and we are to love our neighbors as we love ourselves. Our neighbor is every living person other than ourselves. God calls us to love everyone. All people are our neighbors in God's eyes.

The Fourth Commandment.
Honor your father and your mother.
EXODUS 20:12

The Fourth Commandment teaches us to love the members of our family,

especially our parents. The family is the first and most important group in society. The heart of our family is the love, honor, and respect that bind parents and children. It is our responsibility to deepen this honor and love for as long as we live.

The Fifth Commandment.
You shall not kill.
EXODUS 20:13

The Fifth Commandment teaches us to respect and treat as sacred the life of every person regardless of age, race, gender, health, physical ability, or mental ability. We are to take care of our own life and health and to respect and protect the life and health of others.

The Fifth Commandment also requires us to honor and respect our spiritual life and the spiritual life of others. We are not to scandalize others. This means we are not to deliberately do or say anything that leads people away from their love for God.

What do the Ten Commandments say about buying and playing video games that treat others with acts of violence?

The Sixth and Ninth Commandments.

You shall not commit adultery.

You shall not covet your neighbor's wife.

EXODUS 20:14, 17

God has given each person the gift of being either a boy or a girl who will grow to be a man or a woman. This gift is called our sexuality. The Sixth and Ninth Commandments teach that we are to respect our own sexuality and the sexuality of others. We are to express and share our friendship and love for others in appropriate ways. **Chastity** is the virtue that helps us do this.

The Sixth and Ninth Commandments also teach that the love and life of a husband and wife are sacred, or holy. A husband and wife are to love and honor each other their whole life long.

The Ninth Commandment teaches that other people are to help married people grow in love. They are not to do or say things that tempt married people to be unfaithful or break up a marriage or a family.

Name a popular TV program about friendship or marriage. Give some examples of how that program shows or does not show what the Sixth and Ninth Commandments teach.

_____
(program name)

_____

_____

_____

_____

_____

_____

_____

The Seventh Commandment.

You shall not steal.
EXODUS 20:15

The Seventh Commandment calls us to be people of **justice** and mercy. We are to give God and others what is their due. We are to be generous and kind to others as God is to us. We are to respect and use God's gift of creation wisely. We are to be good stewards of creation.

When we cheat or steal or misuse creation, we are not living as children of God. If we damage things that belong to others, we are to make reparation. We are to return or replace what we have taken or damaged. When we do this, we are acting justly.

The Eighth Commandment.

You shall not bear false witness against your neighbor. EXODUS 20:16

The Eighth Commandment teaches that we are to be people of truth. This means more than not lying. We are to respect the reputation, or good name, of others.

The Tenth Commandment.

You shall not covet your neighbor's goods.
BASED ON EXODUS 20:17

The Tenth Commandment helps us value and respect all the good things that we and other people have as gifts from God. Just as our gifts have been generously given to us by God, we are to share them generously and freely with others—especially with people in need.

List ways you can live a just and truthful life.

Living a Just Life

_____
_____
_____
_____

Living a Truthful Life

_____
_____
_____
_____

United States Conference of Catholic Bishops

The Catholic bishops in the United States help us apply the command to love God and our neighbors to life. One way they do this is through the teachings of the United States Conference of Catholic Bishops (USCCB).

The USCCB was formed in 1966 to guide Catholics in living their faith. The bishops apply the teachings of Jesus to important moral issues in the United States and the world. They have spoken out about nuclear weapons and peace, abortion and capital punishment, economic justice, hunger and fair housing, and the dignity and rights of the elderly and people with disabilities.

The bishops, through the USCCB, help Catholics live as responsible citizens. They remind us of the principles of the Gospel so we can work together to love others justly and with mercy as Jesus taught.

What are some ways you see your parish community building a better world by living the Ten Commandments as Jesus taught?

Our Catholic Identity

Pastoral Letters

The USCCB sometimes writes pastoral letters. Pastoral letters are official statements that the bishops of the USCCB have approved. Pastoral letters present the principles and teachings of the Church on key issues of Catholic living. They guide Catholics in the United States in living their faith according to the teachings of the Church.

What Difference Does Faith Make in My Life?

The Holy Spirit teaches and helps you live the Ten Commandments each day. You pray. You respect and honor your parents and teachers. You treat your classmates and friends with respect. You share with others. You are honest. You are fair and kind to others.

Write a story, draw a picture, or outline a skit that shows ways you and other fifth graders can live the Ten Commandments.

Loving and Respecting Others

My Faith Choice

Each day I have many opportunities to show my love for others as Jesus taught. This week I will

_____

_____.

Prayer of Saint Francis of Assisi

Pray this prayer of Saint Francis. Learn it by heart and pray it each morning.

Lord, make me an instrument of your peace!

Where there is hatred, let me sow love;

where there is injury, pardon;

where there is darkness, light;

where there is doubt, faith;

where there is despair, hope;

where there is sorrow, joy.

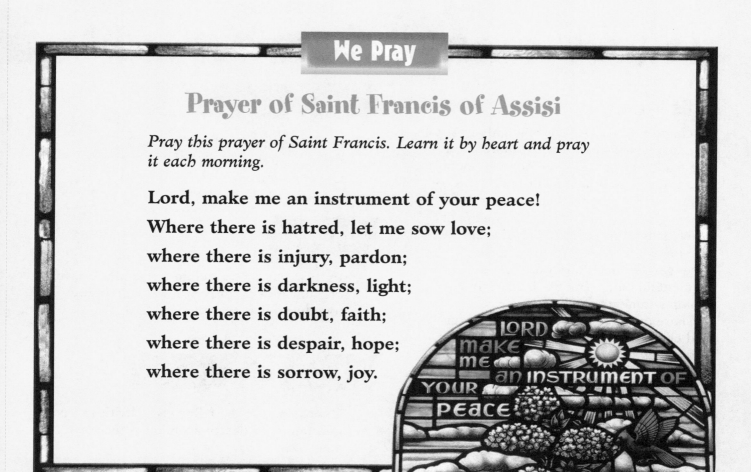

We Remember

Using the Fourth through Tenth Commandments, write the number of the Commandment that names these moral principles.

_____ 1. Respect the gift of sexuality.

_____ 2. Live as a just and honest person.

_____ 3. Respect the good name of others.

_____ 4. Reverence and respect all life.

_____ 5. Share our blessings with others.

_____ 6. Honor and respect parents and those in authority.

_____ 7. Be faithful in marriage.

To Help You Remember

1. The Ten Commandments teach us to honor and respect ourselves and other people.

2. The Ten Commandments teach us to obey and respect our parents and those in authority.

3. The Ten Commandments teach us to be chaste, truthful, just, merciful, kind, and generous.

This Week . . .

In chapter 23, "Love Your Neighbor as Yourself," your child learned more about the teachings of the Ten Commandments. The Fourth Commandment teaches us to honor our parents by respecting and obeying them. The Fifth Commandment teaches us to respect the life of every person as sacred regardless of age, race, gender, health, physical ability, or mental ability. The Sixth and Ninth Commandments teach that we are to share our love for others in a faithful and chaste manner. The Seventh Commandment teaches us to be just and merciful and to use God's creation fairly and wisely. The Eighth Commandment teaches us to live truthful lives. The Tenth Commandment teaches us to respect the good things that we and others have as gifts from God.

For more on the teachings of the Catholic Church on the Fourth through Tenth Commandments, see *Catechism of the Catholic Church* paragraph numbers 2196–2246, 2258–2317, 2331–2391, 2401–2449, 2464–2503, 2514–2527, and 2534–2550.

Sharing God's Word

Read together Matthew 5:17–20. Emphasize that Jesus fulfilled the Commandments.

Praying

In this chapter your child prayed the Prayer of Saint Francis of Assisi. Read and pray together this prayer on page 203.

Making a Difference

Choose one of the following activities to do as a family or design a similar activity of your own.

- The Ten Commandments teach us to honor and respect ourselves and others. How does honoring and respecting others help us grow in faith?

- Watch TV together and keep track of the Commandments that are kept and broken as you watch each show.

- The Fourth Commandment teaches us to honor our mother and father. How does your family honor one another?

For more ideas on ways your family can live your faith, visit the "Faith First for Families" page at **www.FaithFirst.com**. Check out this week's "Just for Parents" article.

Name _____

A. Best Response

Read each statement and circle the best answer.

1. Which one of the following do we not use to make moral decisions?
   - a. intellect
   - b. sin
   - c. free will
   - d. feelings

2. Our conscience helps us to _____.
   - a. encourage people to pray
   - b. read the Bible
   - c. judge what is right and wrong
   - d. develop our ability to think

3. _____ is a moral virtue.
   - a. Fortitude
   - b. Hope
   - c. Love
   - d. Faith

4. In the Beatitudes, peacemakers are called _____.
   - a. children of God
   - b. Apostles
   - c. disciples of Jesus
   - d. members of the Church

5. We have been created in the image and likeness _____.
   - a. of God
   - b. of the angels
   - c. of Adam and Eve
   - d. none of the above

6. "Keep holy the Lord's Day" is the _____ Commandment.
   - a. Fourth
   - b. First
   - c. Third
   - d. Sixth

7. Using God's name with respect is a teaching of the _____ Commandment.
   - a. First
   - b. Eighth
   - c. Fourth
   - d. Second

8. The Eighth Commandment teaches us to _____.
   - a. be people of truth
   - b. honor our parents
   - c. use God's gift of creation wisely
   - d. respect and protect human life as sacred

9. _____ grace is the gift of God sharing his life and love with us.
   - a. Actual
   - b. Sanctifying
   - c. Spiritual
   - d. Christian

10. The First Letter of John reveals that God is _____.
   - a. hope
   - b. love
   - c. forgiveness
   - d. none of the above

B. Matching Words and Phrases

Match the terms in column A with their descriptions
in column B.

Column A

_____ 1. mortal sins

_____ 2. sanctifying grace

_____ 3. love

_____ 4. actual grace

_____ 5. venial sins

Column B

a. God sharing the gift of life and love

b. the gift of God's help to live a holy life

c. sins that separate us from God's love

d. sins that weaken our love for God

e. virtue that helps us keep God at the
   center of our life

C. What I Have Learned

Write three things you learned in this unit. Share
them with the group.

_____

_____

_____

Look at the list of faith terms on page 96. Circle the
terms you know now.

D. From a Scripture Story

What does the First Letter of John teach us about love?
Describe how you can witness John's teachings.

John's Teachings	Witnessing John's Teachings
_____	_____
_____	_____
_____	_____
_____	_____
_____	_____
_____	_____

What kinds of prayers do we pray?

Getting Ready

What I Have Learned

What is something you already know about these faith terms?

The prayer of Jesus

_____

_____

The Church as a people of prayer

_____

_____

The Our Father

_____

_____

Words to Know

Put an X next to the faith terms you know. Put a ? next to the faith terms you need to know more about.

Faith Vocabulary

_____ Psalms

_____ chant

_____ personal prayer

_____ communal prayer

_____ prayer of praise

_____ disciple

Questions I Have

What questions would you like to ask about developing the habit of prayer?

_____

_____

_____

_____

A Scripture Story

Jesus teaching the Our Father

Why does the Church pray the Our Father?

Jesus, Our Model of Prayer

We Pray

Hear my cry, O God,
listen to my prayer!

PSALM 61:2

Lord God, may all
that we do begin and
end in you.   Amen.

*When do you spend time
with your friends?*

Everyone enjoys spending
time with friends. We
enjoy talking with our
friends and doing things
with them. That is what
we do when we pray. We
spend time with God and
share our thoughts and
feelings with him.

*In your own words, describe
what praying means to you.*

The Prayer of the People of God

Faith Focus

What can we learn about prayer from the example of Jesus?

Faith Vocabulary

Psalms. The prayer-songs found in the Old Testament Book of Psalms, or the Psalter.

chant. Plainsong; a simple type of song with only one melody line, using the rhythm of the spoken word.

The Prayer of Jesus

We know from the Gospels that Jesus often prayed. Like all young children, he probably first learned about prayer at home. The teachers in the synagogue in Nazareth and in the Temple in Jerusalem also taught Jesus the prayers of the Jewish people.

Abraham. Jesus would have learned about prayer from the story of Abraham. Abraham listened and followed God when he called him to leave his home and place his trust in him.

Psalms. The **Psalms** share with God the thoughts and feelings of his people. Jesus joined with his family, friends, and neighbors to pray the Psalms.

The Church prays the Psalms every day. Sometimes we **chant**, or sing, the Psalms as King David and the Israelites did. The verses of the responsorial psalm at Mass are often sung this way. We raise up our prayer in song to God.

Think about your day. Create a verse for a psalm that shares your feelings about the day with God.

A page of a fifteenth-century illuminated Bible. This page illustrates Psalm 7 and shows David in prayer.

Woodcarving, artist unknown

Jude Thaddeus

Saint Jude Thaddeus was the cousin of Jesus and the brother of the Apostles Saint James the Lesser and Saint Simon the Zealot. His mother, Mary Clopas, stood by Mary's side at the foot of the cross and anointed the body of Jesus after he died. Many people pray to Saint Jude to help them deal with serious problems that seem impossible to solve. The feast day of Saint Jude, Apostle and martyr, is October 28.

Jesus Prayed Always

There are some times we seem to pray naturally, for example, when someone we care about is sick or something great happens to us. The Gospel writers tell us that when Jesus was about to do something important, he talked it over with his Father. Before choosing the Apostles, Jesus "departed to the mountain to pray, and he spent the night in prayer." When he came down, "he chose Twelve, whom he also named apostles" (Luke 6:12, 13).

Jesus' whole life was a life of prayer. His life, which began in prayer, also ended in prayer. Describing the very moment of Jesus' death, Luke writes:

Jesus cried out in a loud voice, "Father, into your hands I commend my spirit"; and when he had said this he breathed his last.   LUKE 23:46

What times during the day is it important for you to pray? Describe why those times are important.

Trust and Confidence

Jesus showed us that God listens to us when we pray. No matter how long we talk or how often we repeat the same thing, God never stops listening. In the Gospel story about Bartimaeus, the man born blind, Jesus reveals that God always hears and listens to our prayer.

But [Bartimaeus] kept calling out all the more, "Son of David, have pity on me." Jesus stopped and said, "Call him." So they called the blind man, saying to him, "Take courage; get up, he is calling you." He threw aside his cloak, sprang up, and came to Jesus. Jesus said to him in reply, "What do you want me to do for you?" The blind man replied to him, "Master, I want to see." Jesus told him, "Go your way; your faith has saved you." Immediately he received his sight and followed him on the way.

MARK 10:48–52

No one else wanted to listen to Bartimaeus. Jesus stopped, listened, and answered. God always listens. Like Bartimaeus, we trust and have confidence that God always listens to our prayers.

Decorate and learn this prayer by heart. Pray it when you find it difficult to pray.

Jesus Healing the Blind Man, stained glass

Holy Spirit, teach me to pray.

Our Church Makes a Difference

Christian Role Models

Role models help us make good decisions. The saints of the Church are role models whose lives teach us how to make decisions to live our faith. Saints have lived and preached the Gospel in every part of the world. Here are some of the people named saints by Pope John Paul II.

Europe. Edith Stein (1891–1942) was a victim of the Holocaust. She became a Carmelite sister who devoted her life to prayer. Arrested in 1942 she died in the gas chamber at Auschwitz.

Asia. Andrew Dung Lac (1785–1839) and one hundred sixteen others who served the people of Vietnam were martyred by the government of Vietnam.

South America. Born in Paraguay, Roque Gonzalez de Santa Cruz (1576–1628), Alphonsus Rodriquez (1598–1628), and John de Castillo (1596–1628) worked with the tribal people of Paraguay and southern Brazil. They were the first Americans to be beatified as martyrs.

Name a saint who is a role model for you. How can learning about that saint make a difference in the way you live your life?

North America. Rose Philippine Duchesne (1769–1852) came to the United States from France in 1818. She and other members of her religious order worked with orphans and Native Americans. The Potowatami called her "the woman who prays always." Her name is included in the Pioneer Hall of Fame in the state capitol of Missouri.

Saints and people in prayer, tapestry, Cathedral of Our Lady of the Angels, Los Angeles, California

What Difference Does Faith Make in My Life?

Your family and other people have helped you learn to pray. God always listens when you pray.

You learned about some of the most important times in the life of Jesus when he prayed. Describe one important time in your life when you prayed and how praying helped you.

My Life of Prayer

One important time in my life that I have prayed is

_____

_____

_____ .

Praying helped me because

_____

_____

_____ .

My Faith Choice

This week I will spend some time each night thinking about and thanking God for my day.

_____

_____ .

Litany of the Saints

The saints pray for us. Mary is the greatest saint. Think of each of these saints and how much they want you to live as a child of God. Then ask them to pray for you.

Holy Mary, Mother of God,	**pray for us.**
Saint Joseph,	**pray for us.**
Saint John the Baptist,	**pray for us.**
Saint Peter and Saint Paul,	**pray for us.**
Saint Mary Magdalene,	**pray for us.**
Saint John the Evangelist,	**pray for us.**
Saint Agnes,	**pray for us.**
Saint Francis and Saint Dominic,	**pray for us.**
Saint Clare,	**pray for us.**
All holy men and women,	**pray for us.**

We Remember

Circle the words in the puzzle that tell about prayer. Use the words to tell someone why praying is important for you.

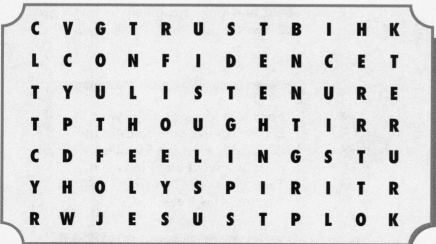

```
C V G T R U S T B I H K
L C O N F I D E N C E T
T Y U L I S T E N U R E
T P T H O U G H T I R R
C D F E E L I N G S T U
Y H O L Y S P I R I T R
R W J E S U S T P L O K
```

To Help You Remember

1. Jesus prayed the Psalms.

2. Jesus prayed before the important events in his life.

3. Jesus showed us that God always listens to our prayers.

This Week . . .

In chapter 24, "Jesus, Our Model of Prayer," your child learned about prayer, especially prayer in the Old Testament and the prayer of Jesus. Jesus' whole life was a life of prayer. Through the help of the Holy Spirit, we lift up our minds and hearts to God and share our thoughts and feelings with him. We pray to God, trusting and confident that he always listens to us and does what is best for us.

For more on the teachings of the Catholic Church on prayer in the Old Testament and the prayer of Jesus, see *Catechism of the Catholic Church* paragraph numbers 2558–2589 and 2598–2617.

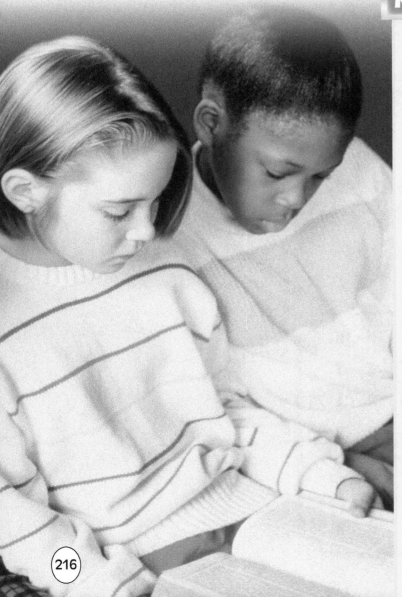

Sharing God's Word

Read together Matthew 6:5–8 and 7:7–11. Emphasize that when we pray we should pray with trust and confidence.

Praying

In this chapter your child prayed part of the Litany of the Saints. Read and pray together the prayer on page 215.

Making a Difference

Choose one of the following activities to do as a family or design a similar activity of your own.

• Pray at the beginning and at the end of each day. Gather in the morning to ask God's blessings on your family. Gather in the evening to thank God for the blessings of the day.

• Saints are our role models. Ask each family member to name a saint who is a role model for them and explain why that saint is a role model.

• Praying can help us make good decisions. Discuss some examples of decisions a family would talk about with God. Talk about how prayer can help us make good decisions.

For more ideas on ways your family can live your faith, visit the "Faith First for Families" page at **www.FaithFirst.com**. Take a look at "Just for Parents" this week.

People of Prayer

We Pray

I rejoiced when they said
  to me,
  "Let us go to the house
  of the LORD."

PSALM 122:1

God, Father, Son,
and Holy Spirit,
we love you, we praise
you, we bless you, we
give you glory.   Amen.

*What is one good habit
you have?*

Good habits come from
doing good things over
and over again. Praying is
a good habit we all need
to develop.

*What are some of your
favorite times and places
to pray?*

Stained-glass window
depicting the Church
as a people of prayer

The Habit of Praying

Praying Always

Prayer is talking and listening to God. It is lifting our minds and hearts up to God alone or together with others.

Sometimes we pray by ourselves. This is called **personal prayer.** We have personal reasons to thank and praise God and personal needs we want to talk about with him. At other times we pray together with other people as a community. This is called **communal prayer.**

We can pray anytime and anyplace. When we make prayer a regular part of our daily lives as Jesus did, we are developing the habit of praying. A good starting point in developing this habit is praying when we wake up each morning. We thank God for bringing us to a new day. We ask God to help us make good choices throughout the day.

Another good time to pray is at mealtimes. Grace before and after meals thanks God for his loving care for us. It is also a prayer asking God to bless people in need.

At the end of our day we thank God for the opportunities that he has given us during the day. We ask God to forgive us for our sins and to protect us and the people we love.

When we pray often, we are doing what Saint Paul the Apostle urges us to do, "Pray without ceasing" (1 Thessalonians 5:17).

List some of the things you can do to develop the habit of praying.

Kinds of Prayer

There are many different kinds of prayers and ways of praying. When we think about what we say in our prayers, we discover that there are five different kinds of prayers. They are prayers of blessing and adoration, prayers of praise, prayers of thanksgiving, prayers of petition, and prayers of intercession.

Every time Christians pray, the Holy Spirit is helping us pray. As members of the Body of Christ, we join our prayer with the prayer of Jesus. We pray to the Father in Jesus' name through the power of the Holy Spirit.

Blessing and adoration. In our prayer of blessing and adoration we tell God he is important to us above all else. He alone is God. We pray:

[L]et us kneel before the LORD who made us.
PSALM 95:6

Praise. Our prayer of praise tells God that we trust in his goodness and greatness and in his love and faithfulness to all people. We pray:

Praise the LORD, all you nations!
PSALM 117:1

Thanksgiving. Our prayer of thanksgiving tells God that he is the source of all that is good. We tell God how much we depend on him. We are grateful to him. We pray:

It is good to give thanks to the LORD.
PSALM 92:2

Petition. Our prayer of sorrow, or contrition, is a prayer of petition. We ask God for the gift of his mercy for having offended him and others. We pray:

Have mercy on me, God, in your goodness.
PSALM 51:3

Intercession. In our prayers of intercession we bring all our needs and the needs of the world to God in prayer. We pray:

May God be gracious to us and bless us.
PSALM 67:2

Faith-Filled People

Pope Gregory I

Saint Gregory I did much to influence the way we celebrate the Mass. Many think that he is the pope who said that the Our Father was to be prayed at every Mass before the breaking of the bread. Some of the music sung at Mass is Gregorian chant, which is named after him. Pope Saint Gregory I is the patron saint of musicians and singers. His feast day is September 3.

Choose one of the five kinds of prayer. Take a moment now and pray, using that kind of prayer.

219

We Pray to Mary

The prayer of Christians is addressed primarily to God the Father, to Jesus, and to the Holy Spirit. Christians also share thoughts and feelings in prayer with Mary and the saints.

Just as children share their thoughts and feelings and needs with their parents, we talk to Mary in prayer. We believe Mary loves and cares for us as a mother loves and cares for her children. We believe that Mary is the Mother of the Church who always welcomes and listens and responds to our prayers.

When we share our thoughts and feelings with Mary, we trust and believe she listens. We believe she shares our prayer with Jesus and asks him to help us.

Write a brief prayer to Mary. Pray your prayer each day.

May crowning, honoring Mary

Our Lady of Guadalupe statue, Saint John the Evangelist Church, Los Angeles, California

Our Church Makes a Difference

Contemplatives

There are religious communities of men and religious communities of women in the Church who dedicate their lives to praying. These religious are called contemplatives. Contemplatives live in convents, monasteries, or abbeys. They organize their day so that everything they do centers around prayer. They set aside times for praying all during the day and night. The work they do to support themselves and the religious community never interferes with the work of praying.

The monks of the Abbey of Gethsemane in Trappist, Kentucky, are contemplatives.

Trappist baking fruit cakes

Trappists in prayer

They gather seven times a day to pray the Liturgy of the Hours, which is the "work of God." In addition, each monk spends time every day prayerfully reading the Scriptures, the writings of the saints, and other writings. All this reading leads to prayer.

The monks of the Abbey of Gethsemane earn their living by making cheese, fruitcake, and fudge. They also care for guests who come there to make a retreat. All the work they do is seen as service.

When does your parish gather to pray? How might your family center its life around prayer?

What Difference Does Faith Make in My Life?

The Holy Spirit teaches and helps you to pray. Remember, you can pray anywhere and anytime.

Complete these sentences to help you discover how easy it is to pray throughout the day.

Growing as a Person of Prayer

I will tell God, "I love you."

I will praise God for _____.

I will thank God for _____.

I will ask God for _____.

My Faith Choice

This week I will try my best to pray several times each day. I will

_____

_____.

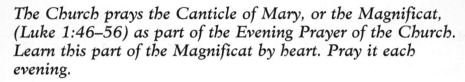

The Magnificat

The Church prays the Canticle of Mary, or the Magnificat, (Luke 1:46–56) as part of the Evening Prayer of the Church. Learn this part of the Magnificat by heart. Pray it each evening.

"My soul proclaims the greatness of the Lord; my spirit rejoices in God my savior."

Luke 1:46–47

We Remember

Use each letter in the word Prayer to describe something about prayer. The letter "Y" has been done for you.

P _____

R _____

A _____

Pray alwaYs _____

E _____

R _____

To Help You Remember

1. Praying throughout the day helps us develop the habit of praying and become people of prayer.

2. The Church prays five different types of prayer: blessing and adoration, praise, thanksgiving, intercession, and petition.

3. Christians pray to Mary, the Mother of the Church.

This Week . . .

In chapter 25, "People of Prayer," your child learned about the importance of developing the habit of praying. The Holy Spirit invites us to pray throughout the day. We pray five basic kinds of prayer—blessing and adoration, praise, thanksgiving, petition, and intercession. The prayer of Christians is primarily addressed to God the Father through the power of the Holy Spirit in the name of Jesus, the Son of God. The Church also prays to Mary, the Mother of the Church, and to the other saints. We are confident and trust that Mary shares our prayers with her Son.

For more on the teachings of the Catholic Church on Christian prayer, see *Catechism of the Catholic Church* paragraph numbers 2623–2643, 2650–2660, and 2663–2677.

Sharing God's Word

Read together Luke 1:46–55, the Canticle of Mary. Emphasize that the Canticle of Mary is a canticle of praise.

Praying

In this chapter your child prayed one verse of Mary's prayer of praise to God, the Magnificat. Read and pray together this prayer on page 223.

Making a Difference

Choose one of the following activities to do as a family or design a similar activity of your own.

- At mealtimes this week think about how God has blessed you. Pray the Magnificat, Mary's prayer of praise to God, for your family mealtime prayer.

- Make a banner with the words "Anywhere, Anytime!" Decorate and hang the banner where it can serve as a reminder to the whole family to pray to God anywhere and anytime.

- Talk about the importance of prayer in the life of a Christian family. Choose one thing you will do this week to make prayer a regular part of every day.

For more ideas on ways your family can live your faith, visit the "Faith First for Families" page at **www.FaithFirst.com**. Click on "Family Prayer," and pray the prayer together this week.

Lord, Teach Us to Pray

A Scripture Story

We Pray

As the heavens tower
  over the earth,
  so God's love towers
  over the faithful.
PSALM 103:11

God, Father and Creator, you are blessed and the source of everything that is good.   Amen.

Who teaches you to pray?

We learn to pray from others. We first learn to pray with our families. Jesus taught his disciples to pray.

When his disciples asked him to teach them to pray, what did Jesus teach them?

Bible Background

Faith Focus

Why do we pray the Our Father?

Faith Vocabulary

disciple. A person who learns from and follows the teachings of another person.

Hillside near the Sea of Galilee

Matthew's Gospel

Mountains had a special meaning to the Jewish people who had become disciples of Jesus. A **disciple** is a person who learns from and follows the teachings of another person. The mountain was a special place of God's presence. It was on a mountain called Mount Sinai that God spoke to Moses and entered into the Covenant with Moses and the Israelites.

In Matthew's Gospel, Jesus teaches his disciples the Our Father on a mountain. This emphasizes how important praying the Our Father is for Christians.

Many believe that the Our Father in Matthew's Gospel was a prayer the early Church had often prayed. Praying the Our Father had become part of what the first Christians did when they gathered for prayer.

Take a moment to pray to God your Father. In the space below write what you would like to share with him.

226

Reading the Word of God

The Our Father

Imagine you are sitting with the disciples on a mountainside and listening to Jesus. You are learning much about what it means to live as his disciple. Then Jesus begins teaching about prayer.

"This is how you are
    to pray:
Our Father in heaven,
    hallowed be your name,
    your kingdom come,
    your will be done
        on earth as in heaven.
Give us today our daily
        bread;
    and forgive us our
        debts,
    as we forgive our
        debtors;
    and do not subject us
        to the final test,
    but deliver us from
        the evil one."

MATTHEW 6:9–13

The Our Father is also called the Lord's Prayer because it is the prayer that Jesus, our Lord, taught us.

Carefully read the words of the Our Father. How does the Our Father help you live as a disciple of Jesus?

Detail from
Christ on the Mountain.
C. Arnold Slade
(1892–1961),
American
painter.

227

A Summary of the Gospel

The Our Father, or Lord's Prayer, has been called the summary of the Gospel. Praying the Our Father teaches us to pray and to live as disciples of Jesus.

OUR FATHER. We do not pray *my* Father but *our* Father. We belong to God as his children. God is our Abba.

WHO ART IN HEAVEN. God, our Father, is glorious and majestic. He is above and beyond everything and everyone else in this world.

HALLOWED BE THY NAME. *Hallowed* means "very holy" and "very honored." We want all the peoples of the world to know and love God, the Creator and Redeemer of the universe.

THY KINGDOM COME. We live in hope and wait with trust for the day when God's kingdom of justice and peace, of love and wisdom announced by Jesus will completely take hold of our world.

THY WILL BE DONE. God's will is that all will be saved in Jesus. We pray that we will follow God's will and live as Jesus taught us to live.

GIVE US THIS DAY OUR DAILY BREAD. Each day and every moment of our lives we depend on God to give us life. We place our trust in him.

FORGIVE US OUR TRESPASSES AS WE FORGIVE THOSE WHO TRESPASS AGAINST US. We ask God to forgive us. We promise to forgive all people who hurt us.

LEAD US NOT INTO TEMPTATION, BUT DELIVER US FROM EVIL. We ask God's grace to overcome whatever and whoever would separate us from him.

At Mass we conclude the Our Father by praying, "for the kingdom, the power, and the glory are yours, now and forever." How do you give glory to God?

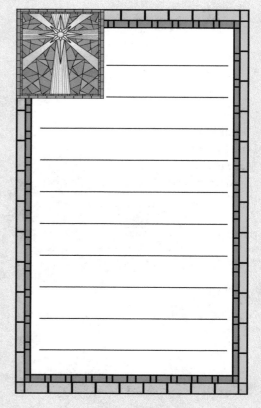

Young volunteers helping to gather green sea turtle eggs

Our Catholic Identity

Evangelization

God has made the Church the steward of the Gospel. The most important responsibility of the Church is to care for and share with all people the good news of God's love that he has shared with us in Jesus Christ. We call this work of the Church evangelization, or sharing the good news.

Caring for God's Creation

When we call God our Father, we are showing that all creation belongs to him. God has given us the responsibility to care for one another and for the world. This responsibility includes the responsibility to use creation to do the work of God and give glory to him.

We are to be good stewards of God's creation. A steward is someone who has responsibility to care for what belongs to someone else.

How are the people in the pictures acting as good stewards of creation?

What Difference Does Faith Make in My Life?

Each time you pray the Our Father, the Holy Spirit helps you grow as a child of God. You learn both how to pray and how to live the Gospel.

Write or draw something you could do to help others understand that God is the Father of all people.

God Is Our Father

My Faith Choice

This week I will think about how I can act more like a son or daughter of God, our Abba, the loving Father of all people. I will

_____

_____.

The Lord's Prayer

The Our Father, or Lord's Prayer, is the prayer of all Christians. Pray it every day.

Leader: Jesus prayed, "Father, I pray that they all may be one, as we are one."

BASED ON JOHN 17:20–22

Together, let us join hands and pray as Jesus taught us:

All: **Our Father . . .**

Leader: Let us share a sign of peace to show that we are all children of God, our Father.

We Remember

Imagine that you were on the mountain listening as Jesus taught the disciples the Our Father. Create a headline and write a news report describing what happened. See how many of these words and phrases you can include in your report.

mountain	Lord's Prayer	worship
hallowed	trust	God the Father
forgive	justice	children love

To Help You Remember

1. Jesus taught his disciples to pray the Our Father.

2. The Our Father teaches us how to pray.

3. The Our Father teaches us how to live the Gospel.

_____

_____

_____

_____

_____

_____

This Week . . .

In chapter 26, "Lord, Teach Us to Pray: A Scripture Story," your child learned about the Our Father. In Matthew's Gospel, Jesus' teaching the Our Father, or Lord's Prayer, to the disciples is part of the Sermon on the Mount. Many biblical scholars think that the version of the Our Father in Matthew's Gospel is close to the version the early Church prayed. The Lord's Prayer has been called the summary of the Gospel. When we pray the Our Father, the Holy Spirit teaches us both how to pray and how to live the Gospel.

For more on the teaching of the Catholic Church on the Our Father, see *Catechism of the Catholic Church* paragraph numbers 2759–2856.

Sharing God's Word

Read together Matthew 6:9–13 on page 227 or in a Bible. Emphasize that the Our Father is also called the Lord's Prayer because it is the prayer that Jesus, our Lord, taught us.

Praying

In this chapter your child prayed the Lord's Prayer. Read and pray together the prayer on page 231.

Making a Difference

Choose one of the following activities to do as a family or design a similar activity of your own.

- When you participate in Mass this week, pay close attention to the praying of the Lord's Prayer. Be sure to pray every word of this special prayer.

- Jesus reminds us that God is our Father. Every member of your family is a child of God. Choose one thing you can do this week to live as God's children.

- Use the Lord's Prayer for family prayer this week.

For more ideas on ways your family can live your faith, visit the "Faith First for Families" page at **www.FaithFirst.com**. "Gospel Reflections" will continue to change each week over the summer. Don't forget to check it out.

Unit 4 Review

Name _____

A. Best Response

Read each statement and circle the best answer.

1. Jesus prayed the ____ .
   - a. Psalms
   - b. Nicene Creed
   - c. Apostles' Creed
   - d. Hail Mary

2. Jesus taught us to pray ____ .
   - a. with trust
   - b. with confidence
   - c. out of love
   - d. all of the above

3. Jesus taught his disciples the ____ .
   - a. Glory Prayer
   - b. Creed
   - c. Our Father
   - d. Act of Contrition

4. Asking God to forgive us is a prayer of ____ .
   - a. praise
   - b. thanksgiving
   - c. petition
   - d. adoration

5. A prayer of ____ tells God that he alone is God.
   - a. praise
   - b. intercession
   - c. blessing and adoration
   - d. thanksgiving

6. A prayer of ____ tells God that he is the source of all that is good.
   - a. praise
   - b. intercession
   - c. blessing and adoration
   - d. thanksgiving

7. A prayer of ____ tells God we trust in his faithfulness.
   - a. praise
   - b. intercession
   - c. blessing and adoration
   - d. thanksgiving

8. ____ prayer is praying with other people.
   - a. Communal
   - b. Personal
   - c. Private
   - d. Daily

9. The prayer of Christians is addressed primarily to ____ .
   - a. Mary
   - b. God the Father
   - c. the saints
   - d. the Holy Spirit

10. The Our Father is a summary of the ____ .
    - a. Ten Commandments
    - b. Gospel
    - c. Creed
    - d. sacraments

B. Matching Words and Phrases

Match the parts of the Lord's Prayer in column A
with their descriptions in column B.

Column A

_____ 1. Our Father who art
in heaven

_____ 2. Hallowed be thy name

_____ 3. Thy will be done

_____ 4. Give us this day
our daily bread

_____ 5. Forgive us our
trespasses as we
forgive those who
trespass against us

Column B

a. God is glorious beyond all that
he has created.

b. We ask God to forgive us and we
forgive others.

c. We pray that we will always do
what God wants us to do.

d. We depend on God each day.

e. God's name is holy and honored.

C. What I Have Learned

Write three things you learned in this unit.
Share them with the group.

_____

_____

_____

Look at the list of faith terms in "Words to Know" on
page 208. Circle the terms that you know now.

D. From a Scripture Story

The Book of Psalms contains prayers of praise, blessing and
adoration, thanksgiving, petition, and intercession. Choose two
of these kinds of prayers. Write your own psalm verse for each.

_____   _____

_____   _____

_____   _____

_____   _____

Why are the celebrations of the Church's liturgical year important?

The Liturgical Year

The Year of the Lord

From the earliest days of the Church, the Church has celebrated Sunday as the Lord's Day.

The Church celebrates the paschal mystery on the first day of the week, known as the Lord's Day or Sunday. This follows a tradition handed down from the apostles and having its origin from the day of Christ's resurrection. Thus Sunday must be ranked as the first holyday of all.

ROMAN MISSAL, "GENERAL NORMS FOR THE LITURGICAL YEAR AND THE CALENDAR," 4

In addition to the celebration of Sunday, the Church celebrates a cycle of seasons, solemnities, feasts, and memorials. The lessons in this unit focus on the seasons of the liturgical year. This page lists the solemnities and feasts of Jesus and of Mary that the Church in the United States of America celebrates throughout the year.

Solemnities and Feasts of Jesus Christ

Epiphany
Sunday between January 2 and January 8

Baptism of the Lord
Sunday after Epiphany

Presentation of the Lord
February 2

Annunciation
March 25

The Body and Blood of Christ
Sunday after Holy Trinity

Sacred Heart
Friday following Second Sunday after Pentecost

Transfiguration
August 6

Triumph of the Cross
September 14

Christ the King
Last Sunday in Ordinary Time

Christmas
December 25

Solemnities, Feasts, and Memorials of the Blessed Virgin Mary

Mary, Mother of God
January 1

Our Lady of Lourdes
February 11

Visitation
May 31

Immaculate Heart of Mary
Saturday following Second Sunday after Pentecost

Our Lady of Mount Carmel
July 16

Assumption
August 15

Queenship of Mary
August 22

Birth of Mary
September 8

Our Lady of Sorrows
September 15

Our Lady of the Rosary
October 7

Presentation of Mary
November 21

Immaculate Conception
December 8

Our Lady of Guadalupe
December 12

Faith Focus

How does celebrating Ordinary Time help us grow as Christians?

The Word of the Lord

These are the Gospel readings for the Third Sunday in Ordinary Time. Choose this year's reading. Read and discuss it with your family.

Year A
  Matthew 4:12–23
    or
  Matthew 4:12–17
Year B
  Mark 1:14–20
Year C
  Luke 1:1–4
    or
  Luke 4:14–21

The Church's Year of Worship

While many things you see and hear at Mass are the same each Sunday, some things are different. You listen to readings that are different each week. You join with others in singing hymns that often change. Throughout the year you will notice that the color of the banners and the vestments of the priest and other ministers also changes. At times during the year the Church is filled with flowers and decorations; at other times it is not.

All these changes help us know what part of the Church's year we are celebrating. We call the yearly cycle of celebrating the liturgy the liturgical year.

The Seasons of the Church's Year

Advent, Christmas, Lent, Easter, and Ordinary Time are the main seasons of the Church's liturgical year. The Triduum, which includes Holy Thursday, Good Friday, and the Easter Vigil/Easter Sunday, is the center of the liturgical year.

When you take part in Mass, you will notice that sometimes the vestments of the priest and deacon are green. Green vestments are worn during Ordinary Time. This is the longest part of the Church's liturgical year.

If it is the longest part of the year, why would the Church call it "Ordinary" Time? Well, it is not ordinary in the way you might first think. The name *ordinary* comes from a Latin word that means "number."

Each Sunday of Ordinary Time is identified by a number, as in the "Twenty-fifth Sunday of the Year." All throughout Ordinary Time we are celebrating a very important work. Each week in the Liturgy of the Word, we remember and listen to the teachings and work of Jesus. Just as Jesus' listeners sat on the mountainside or stood in the marketplace or walked with him along the roads of Galilee or the streets in Jerusalem, we listen and watch too. We think about what Jesus is saying and doing. We learn about what it means to live as a Christian in our own homes, in schools, and in our communities.

Celebrating Our Catholic Faith

You join with the Church to celebrate the liturgy throughout the year. In the wheel write one way you can follow Jesus in each part of the liturgical year.

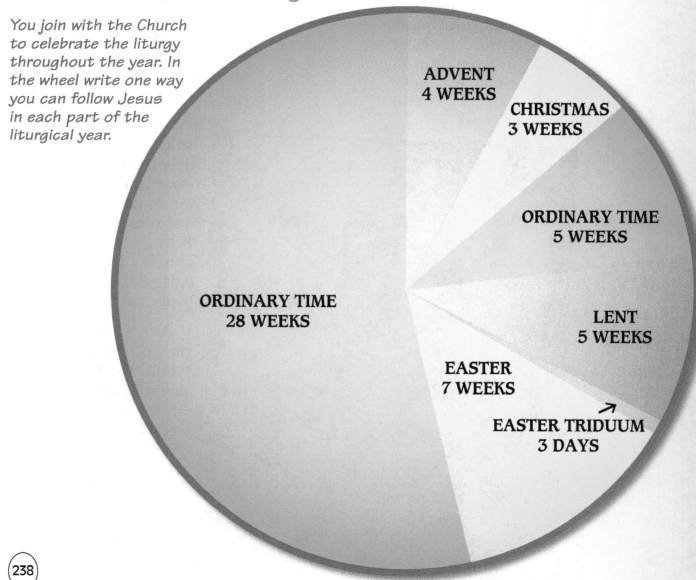

ADVENT
4 WEEKS

CHRISTMAS
3 WEEKS

ORDINARY TIME
5 WEEKS

ORDINARY TIME
28 WEEKS

LENT
5 WEEKS

EASTER
7 WEEKS

EASTER TRIDUUM
3 DAYS

Faith Focus

What does the season of Advent help us to prepare for?

The Word of the Lord

These are the Gospel readings for the First Sunday of Advent. Choose this year's reading. Read and discuss it with your family.

Year A
Matthew 24:37–44

Year B
Mark 13:33–37

Year C
Luke 21:25–28, 34–36

What You See

The Advent wreath is made of evergreens with four candles. The candles are lighted successively each week of Advent to symbolize the coming of Christ, the Light of the world.

Preparing for the Coming of the Lord

New things happen all the time. In the spring we see new life everywhere. In school we learn new things every day. Watching TV we learn things about the world we never knew before.

Advent begins a new year for Christians. It is a new year and a new time to renew our love for God and for one another. It is a time to accept the Holy Spirit's invitation and grace to prepare ourselves to make room in our hearts for Jesus.

John the Baptist announced, "Prepare the way for the Lord." During the four weeks of Advent we do just that. We listen to the Scripture readings each Sunday and are reminded to prepare for the coming of the Lord in our lives. For the Lord not only came on that first Christmas but also comes to us every moment of every day. He will come again in glory at the end of time.

During Advent we welcome Jesus into our lives every day. Then we will truly be ready to welcome him with great joy at Christmas.

Lighting the Advent wreath on the Third Sunday of Advent

Awaiting the Lord's Coming

*Look up these stories in your Bible. Each is about a person
whose words and example help prepare us for the Lord's coming.
In the spaces write the name of the person in each story.*

Read Mark 1:1–8. **Who first used the words:
"Behold, I am sending my messenger ahead
of you; / he will prepare your way"?** MARK 1:2

_____

Read Luke 1:46–56. **Who said yes to God and sang
these words: "My soul proclaims the greatness
of the Lord"?** LUKE 1:46

_____

Read Matthew 1:18–25. **Who believed Isaiah's words:
"Behold, the virgin shall be with child and bear a son, /
and they shall name him Emmanuel"?** MATTHEW 1:23

_____

Read Matthew 3:1–7. **Who announced Jesus' coming
and preached repentance by saying: "Prepare the way
of the Lord"?** MATTHEW 3:3

_____

Faith Focus

How does listening to the story of Saint John the Baptist help us celebrate Advent?

The Word of the Lord

These are the Gospel readings for the Second Sunday of Advent. Choose this year's reading. Read and discuss it with your family.

Year A
  Matthew 3:1–12

Year B
  Mark 1:1–8

Year C
  Luke 3:1–6

Prepare the Way!

The lights go down. The music begins to roar and fills the arena. The voice of the announcer is loud and clear. Quickly, the spirit of the hometown crowd is raised. The players are introduced one by one as we cheer. The announcer has done his job. We are prepared.

Saint John the Baptist was the son of Elizabeth and Zechariah. At the birth of John, his father sang a canticle, or song of praise, to describe the work his son would do. Zechariah said:

"And you, child, will be called prophet of the Most High, for you will go before the Lord to prepare his ways, to give his people knowledge of salvation." LUKE 1:76–77

When John grew up, he went into the desert to prepare to do his work. One day he came down to the banks of the Jordan River and announced the coming of the Messiah. The Messiah was the One whom God had promised to send to save his people. John preached, "Turn back to God and change your ways." Many listened to John and changed their ways.

Telling Others About Jesus

Many people help you come to know Jesus Christ. When they do, they are like John the Baptist. In this space draw or write an announcement that will help others come to know Jesus.

How does listening to the message of the prophet Isaiah help us celebrate Advent?

The Word of the Lord

These are the Gospel readings for the Third Sunday of Advent. Choose this year's reading. Read and discuss it with your family.

Year A
   Matthew 11:2–11

Year B
   John 1:6–8, 19–28

Year C
   Luke 3:10–18

God's Promised One

In times past, God chose certain people to speak in his name. We call these people prophets. The writings of Isaiah the Prophet are often read during Advent.

Isaiah spoke many wonderful words that filled people's hearts with hope. As they were suffering at the hands of the Assyrians, who were trying to conquer the world, God's people wanted a leader who would help them survive. Isaiah promised that God would send a leader to help them.

This is how the Book of Isaiah describes this new leader:

The spirit of the LORD shall
   rest upon him:
a spirit of wisdom and
   of understanding,
A spirit of counsel and of
   strength,
a spirit of knowledge and
   of fear of the LORD.
                    ISAIAH 11:2

But he shall judge the
   poor with justice,
   and decide aright for
   the land's afflicted. . . .
Justice shall be the band
   around his waist,
   and faithfulness a belt
   upon his hips. . . .
There shall be no harm or
   ruin on all my holy
   mountain;
   for the earth shall be
   filled with knowledge
   of the LORD,
   as water covers the sea.
                ISAIAH 11:4, 5, 9

Isaiah was speaking about Jesus. Jesus is the Promised One who Isaiah said would bring peace to all people. When Jesus began his work on earth, he went into the synagogue and read from the writings of Isaiah. When he finished reading, he rolled up the scroll and announced that he was the One Isaiah spoke about many years ago.

Jesus, God's Promised One

Look at the example. The first symbol is ⬚. Find this shape ⬚ on the grid. Notice that the dot is in the first position. This means that G is the first letter. Work through the O and D. Now decode this message from Isaiah the Prophet.

Example: G   o   d

ABC	JKL	STU
DEF	MNO	VWX
GHI	PQR	YZ

"___ ___ ___ ___   ___ ___ ___ ___ ___

___ ___ ___ ___   ___ ___ ___

___ ___ ___ ___ ___ ___ ___ ___

___ ___ ___ ___ ___ ___ ___ ___ ___." MATTHEW 1:23

Faith Focus

How do the words and actions of Mary help us celebrate Advent?

The Word of the Lord

These are the Gospel readings for the Fourth Sunday of Advent. Choose this year's reading. Read and discuss it with your family.

Year A
   Matthew 1:18–24

Year B
   Luke 1:26–38

Year C
   Luke 1:39–45

Hill country near Nazareth, showing the type of land Mary would have traveled to visit Elizabeth

Mary's Song of Joy

When something exciting happens to us, we cannot wait to share it. When friends begin to tell us about something good that has happened to them, we cannot wait to hear more about it. That is just how Elizabeth, the mother of John the Baptist, and Mary felt before their sons were born.

Mary and Elizabeth both believed they were very blessed by God. Through both their children, God would fulfill his promises to his people. The time God's people were waiting for had finally come.

We listen carefully each Advent as we retell the story of Mary and Elizabeth as they prepare for the birth of their sons. The Gospel according to Luke tells us that the angel Gabriel announced to Mary that her child "will be called holy, the Son of God" (Luke 1:35). At the same time, Gabriel told Mary that Elizabeth, her relative, was going to have a child too. Hearing that news, Mary traveled into the hill country to visit Elizabeth.

245

Seeing Mary approaching her home, Elizabeth praised God for blessing Mary. She greeted Mary, saying, "Most blessed are you among women, and blessed is the fruit of your womb. . . . Blessed are you who believed that what was spoken to you by the Lord would be fulfilled" (Luke 1:42, 45). During Advent, Christians throughout the world remember this event. In languages spoken throughout the whole world we praise and thank God the Father for sending his only Son to come to live among us.

God Among Us

Complete the sentences to show your belief that God truly does live among us. The first two sentences have already been completed.

We recognize you in the poor and the homeless.

We recognize you when someone helps us know you better.

We recognize you in _____

_____

_____.

We recognize you when _____

_____

_____.

We recognize you where _____

_____

_____.

Faith Focus

Why do we say that Jesus is the Prince of Peace?

The Word of the Lord

These are the Gospel readings for Mass on Christmas Day. Choose one reading. Read and discuss it with your family.

John 1:1–18 or
John 1:1–5, 9–14

What You See

Evergreen trees and wreaths are Christmas symbols. The circle of the evergreen wreath is a sign of God's never-ending love for us.

Shout for Joy!

Imagine a world filled with peace and harmony. Think of a world in which no families are homeless and all children eat well each and every day. What would that world be like? The Son of God became one of us and lived among us to show us how to build such a world. It is a task we will need to work at until Jesus comes again at the end of time.

During the Christmas season we remember and celebrate that "a savior has been born for you who is Messiah and Lord" (Luke 2:11). Joining with the angels, we sing:

"Glory to God in the highest / and on earth peace to those on whom his favor rests." LUKE 2:14

We proclaim Jesus is the Prince of Peace, who makes all things new. Announcing the kingdom of peace, Isaiah says:

The calf and the young lion shall browse together,
with a little child to guide them.

ISAIAH 11:6

When Jesus was born, God's plan for all people to live in peace was born again too. All creatures, even those who now treat each other as enemies, are called to live together in peace. Jesus is the Prince of Peace. With him we work to build a world of peace. We prepare for the coming of the kingdom of God.

Making All Things New

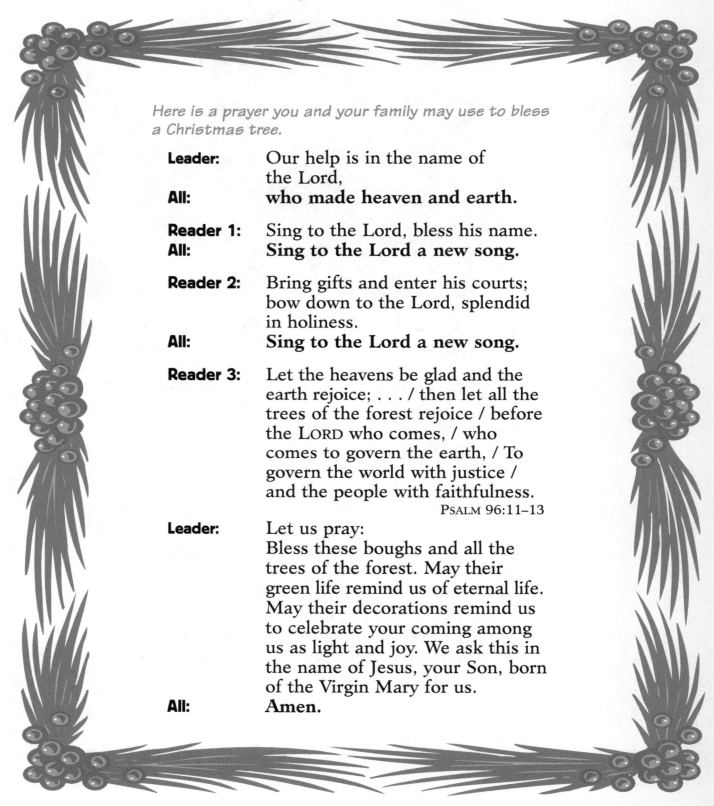

Here is a prayer you and your family may use to bless a Christmas tree.

Leader: Our help is in the name of the Lord,

All: **who made heaven and earth.**

Reader 1: Sing to the Lord, bless his name.

All: **Sing to the Lord a new song.**

Reader 2: Bring gifts and enter his courts; bow down to the Lord, splendid in holiness.

All: **Sing to the Lord a new song.**

Reader 3: Let the heavens be glad and the earth rejoice; . . . / then let all the trees of the forest rejoice / before the LORD who comes, / who comes to govern the earth, / To govern the world with justice / and the people with faithfulness.

PSALM 96:11–13

Leader: Let us pray:
Bless these boughs and all the trees of the forest. May their green life remind us of eternal life. May their decorations remind us to celebrate your coming among us as light and joy. We ask this in the name of Jesus, your Son, born of the Virgin Mary for us.

All: **Amen.**

Faith Focus

Why does the Church share with us stories about the Holy Family?

The Word of the Lord

This is the second reading for the Second Sunday of Christmas. Read and discuss it with your family.

Ephesians 1:3–6, 15–18

What You See

During the Christmas season the color of the vestments is white. White is the symbol for the fullness of life. The Christmas season celebrates that Jesus is the source of the fullness of life for all people.

The Flight into Egypt. Johannes Guntmann, nineteenth-century Austrian artist.

Faith Stories of Our Church

Our families like to tell stories about us. Their love for us is so great that they want friends and relatives to know all about us. Our family stories tell people who we are and what is important to us.

Our Church also has stories to tell. We tell these stories over and over again, year after year. During the Christmas season we share many of the New Testament stories about Jesus as a child. These stories help us understand what the Church believes about Jesus. Here are two of the stories.

The Presentation in the Temple

Shortly after Jesus' birth, Joseph and Mary brought Jesus to the Temple in Jerusalem. There Anna and Simeon greeted the Holy Family. Both Anna and Simeon were elderly and had been waiting for the fulfillment of the Old Testament hopes and promises. Holding the infant Jesus in his arms, Simeon proclaimed:

"Now, Master, you may let your servant go
in peace, according to your word,
for my eyes have seen your salvation." LUKE 2:29–30

The Journey into Egypt

Some time after Jesus' birth, an angel warned Joseph that Jesus' life was in danger and directed him to take Mary and Jesus to Egypt. The Holy Family fled to Egypt and lived there just as God's people in the Old Testament had done. When the danger was over, God told Joseph to return home with the Holy Family. When the early Church heard this story, it probably reminded them of the story of God telling Moses to lead his people out of Egypt.

These and other stories tell us that Jesus is the Messiah. Jesus is the center of the story of God's love for all people. He is the Promised One sent by God for the salvation of the world.

Remembering the Child Jesus

For years you have listened to the stories of Jesus' birth and childhood. Look up each Bible passage. Make notes for yourself. Then retell the Bible story in your own words.

Matthew 2:13–18 _____

_____

_____

Matthew 2:19–23 _____

_____

_____

Luke 2:22–38 _____

_____

_____

Luke 2:41–52 _____

_____

_____

_____

_____

The First Week of Lent

Faith Focus

Why do we call Lent the Church's springtime?

The Word of the Lord

These are the Gospel readings for the First Sunday of Lent. Choose this year's reading. Read and discuss it with your family.

Year A
   Matthew 4:1–11

Year B
   Mark 1:12–15

Year C
   Luke 4:1–13

What You See

During Lent the color of the vestments is purple or violet. Purple is a symbol of sorrow and penance. We remember Jesus' Passion and prepare to celebrate his Resurrection.

The Church's Springtime

Spring is a season of rebirth and renewal. During springtime flowers begin to grow. Leaves begin to sprout and cover the bare branches of winter. Ice and snow begin to melt. Flowing down mountainsides, streams fill the forests with sounds of new life. Nature begins its long return from death to new life.

Lent is the Church's sacred springtime. It is a season of rebirth and renewal. It is the time when people make final preparations to receive new life in Christ in Baptism. It is a time that the baptized renew the new life we have received in Baptism.

During Lent we walk with Jesus and stand with him as we meditate on his Passion and death. Lent is also a time when we look forward to the Resurrection at Easter.

During Lent we strengthen our decision to be faithful to the Great Commandment, which calls us to love God and love our neighbor as ourselves. We make decisions that increase our efforts to

- give alms, or share our time, talents, and other gifts with which God has blessed us;
- fast, or eat less, and share in the sufferings of Jesus; and
- pray, or talk things over with God more often.

Throughout Lent we not only make private decisions to fulfill our baptismal promise. We also join with other members of the Church to work and pray together. We support one another in our celebration of Lent. We look forward to Easter and the celebration of our new life in Christ.

Finding Out About the Season of Lent

Find a classmate who can help you complete these statements about Lent. Write your answers in the spaces provided and have your classmate put his or her initials on the lines.

The color used to celebrate Lent is

_____. Initials:_____

A Lenten devotion is

_____. Initials:_____

Lent lasts this many days:

_____ Initials:_____

Lent begins on

_____. Initials:_____

Lent ends on

_____. Initials:_____

Lent is a season of

_____. Initials:_____

(253)

Faith Focus

How does the Church renew and prepare for Baptism during Lent?

The Word of the Lord

These are the Gospel readings for the Second Sunday of Lent. Choose this year's reading. Read and discuss it with your family.

Year A
    Matthew 17:1–9

Year B
    Mark 9:2–10

Year C
    Luke 9:28–36

What You Hear

Before the Gospel reading, the Alleluia is sung in every season except Lent. During Lent only a Psalm verse is used before the reading of the Gospel.

Baptismal Commitment

Baptism celebrates your birthday as a Christian. Through Baptism you were joined to Christ and became a member of his Church.

As we listen to the Scripture readings during Lent, we hear many images that describe Jesus. He is "living water," "the light of the world," and "the resurrection and the life."

These images help us understand our Baptism and what it means to be a member of the Body of Christ, the Church.

We call the Body of Christ that has gathered for worship the worshiping assembly. The assembly is divided into three groups of people:
- the faithful,
- penitents, and
- catechumens.

The faithful are the baptized members of the Church who seek to renew themselves. The penitents are those who have separated themselves from the Church and who seek to return to the Church once again. The catechumens are those who seek to become members of the Church. For them Lent is a time to prepare for the celebration of the Sacraments of Initiation—Baptism, Confirmation, and Eucharist.

Throughout Lent all the members of the Church pray for and help one another. Together we renew our life in Christ and prepare to celebrate our newness of life in him at Easter.

Supporting One Another During Lent

During Lent you join with your parish to help the catechumens prepare for their initiation into the Church. In this space create a message you could share with the catechumens in your parish.

_____

_____

_____

_____

_____

_____

_____

_____

_____

_____

Faith Focus

How does prayer help the Church renew and prepare for Baptism during Lent?

The Word of the Lord

These are the Gospel readings for the Third Sunday of Lent. Choose this year's reading. Read and discuss it with your family.

Year A
John 4:5–42 or
John 4:5–15,
    19–26, 39,
    40–44

Year B
John 2:13–25

Year C
Luke 13:1–9

Listening to God

Think about the many ways you like to pray. You can pray alone or with others. You can pray aloud or quietly in your heart.

God has revealed that he is always near. He is always at our side, listening to us and waiting for us to speak to him. This is what praying is really all about—talking and listening to God.

Lent is a special time for growing as a person of prayer. During Lent we think about the many stories in the Bible that tell about God's forgiveness. As we listen to God's word, we ask him to forgive our sins and to help us make better decisions to live as followers of Jesus Christ. Praying the word of God, alone or with other people, helps us open our hearts to God.

Making a special effort to read and pray using the Bible is very important. Scripture tells us, "Be still before the LORD; / wait for God" (Psalm 37:7). Praying Scripture keeps us, in a special way, in his presence. We try to be still and become more aware of God's presence with us. We can listen to the Holy Spirit, who lives in our heart and speaks to us.

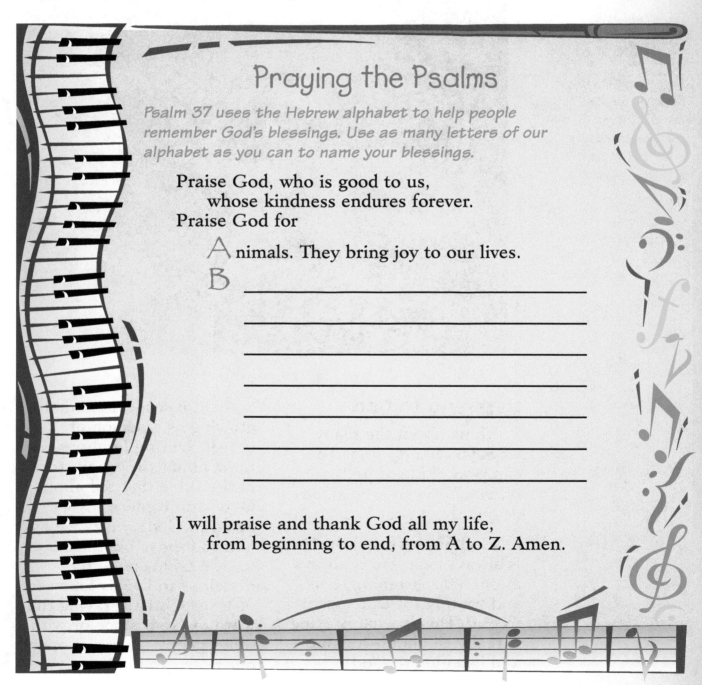

Praying the Psalms

Psalm 37 uses the Hebrew alphabet to help people remember God's blessings. Use as many letters of our alphabet as you can to name your blessings.

Praise God, who is good to us,
    whose kindness endures forever.
Praise God for

A nimals. They bring joy to our lives.

B _____

_____

_____

_____

_____

_____

I will praise and thank God all my life,
    from beginning to end, from A to Z. Amen.

Faith Focus

How does Lent help us remember to live as followers of Jesus?

These are the Gospel readings for the Fourth Sunday of Lent. Choose this year's reading. Read and discuss it with your family.

Year A
John 9:1–41 or John 9:1, 6–9, 13–17, 34–38

Year B
John 3:14–21

Year C
Luke 15:1–3, 11–32

As we get closer to remembering the time of Jesus' suffering and death, the music we hear becomes less joyful.

Changing to Do Better

Most of us like to learn new words. Here is a new word—*metanoia*. It means "a change of heart." You often have to change the way you do something to learn to do it better. For example, if you learn how to take better notes, you study better. What have you changed that has helped you do something better?

During Lent the Church helps us live the Gospel better. One thing we try to do is work harder at being more generous with the gifts God has given us. We look at the ways we may be treating others selfishly and treat them as we want them to treat us. Remembering that God is merciful and gracious, we try to be kinder and more forgiving.

We also look at how we are using and caring for creation. We turn away from using resources and creatures of the world carelessly. We work harder at becoming more careful in our use of water, food, and the other gifts of the earth.

Jesus told us that we are to be lights in the world. During Lent we think more about ways to do this. When we are self-giving and generous, we are filled with the light and love of God. We are letting our light shine as Jesus asked.

Lights in the World

LEADER: Dear brothers and sisters, as we continue to celebrate Lent, let us consider how we can live as lights in the world.

READER 1: God made all things and shares his life and love with us.

ALL: **Let us live as lights in the world.**

READER 2: God asks that we learn to live the Gospel better.

ALL: **Let us live as lights in the world.**

LEADER: Take out a small piece of paper. Write down one action that will help you live as a light in the world. *(Pause.)* Let us pray:

READER 3: In our need, Spirit of God,

ALL: **be our helper.**

READER 4: In our weakness, Spirit of God,

ALL: **be our power.**

READER 5: In our life as followers of Christ, Spirit of God,

ALL: **be our life, now and forever more. Amen!**

Faith Focus

Why is the cross of Christ central to our celebration of Lent?

The Word of the Lord

These are the Gospel readings for the Fifth Sunday of Lent. Choose this year's reading. Read and discuss it with your family.

Year A
    John 11:1–45 or
    John 11:3–7, 17,
        20–27,
        33–45

Year B
    John 12:20–33

Year C
    John 8:1–11

Remembering the Passion and Death of Jesus

Sometimes bad things happen to us. These things might hurt our feelings or harm our bodies or both. But sometimes something good comes out of a bad experience. You may fail a test, but good can come out of your failing. This experience can encourage you to work harder to learn more and do better on the next test.

From Jesus' death on the cross came new life. Lent helps us remember that we share in the new life that came out of Jesus' suffering and death.

Christians give the cross a place of honor in our churches and in our lives. During Lent, Catholics put aside time to kneel before the crucifix and thank God for his great love for us. On the Fridays of Lent, many parish communities pray the Stations of the Cross. On their own, some people set aside a time to walk with Jesus and meditate on his journey to death and through his death to his Resurrection. We look at our own life and ask, "How are we sharing in Jesus' suffering and in his Resurrection?"

Youth praying the Stations of the Cross during World Youth Day, Denver, Colorado

Follow Me

As the youth columnist for your local Catholic newspaper, you receive these letters in the mail. How would you answer them?

I play the flute pretty well. Our parish wants musicians to play during Holy Week. I don't think I'm good enough. What do you think?

Deaundra Flutist

Dear Deaundra,

My grandpa wants me to come and visit him. He is lonely, but he tells the same stories over and over and over. How can I get out of this?

Jason Bored

Dear Jason,

I love chocolate! I gave it up for Lent, but I ate a whole bag of chocolate-covered peanuts last night. Now that I've eaten chocolate, why should I continue to give it up?

Failing Pepe

Dear Pepe,

Dear Huan Yue,

I ruined my friend's CD. I don't have any money to get her a new one. What can I do? I really want to wait until I have the money before I tell her.

Puzzled Huan Yue

Palm Sunday of the Lord's Passion

Faith Focus

Why do we say that Holy Week is a celebration of being forgiven and growing in forgiveness?

The Word of the Lord

These are the Gospel readings for Palm Sunday of the Lord's Passion. Choose this year's reading. Read and discuss it with your family.

Year A
   Matthew 26:14–27:66 or
   Matthew 27:11–54

Year B
   Mark 14:1–15:47 or
   Mark 15:1–39

Year C
   Luke 22:14–23:56 or
   Luke 23:1–49

What You See

Palm branches are blessed and carried in procession and are held high as we listen to the reading of "The Passion of our Lord Jesus Christ."

A Forgiven and a Forgiving People

Forgiving others and being forgiven by others are two very important things. A forgiving word or look, a hug or a smile for someone who has been hurt helps families grow closer. An apology to someone we have hurt can make a friendship stronger. Forgiveness, reconciliation, and new life are what the life and work of Jesus were all about.

Holy Week begins the center of the story of God's plan of forgiveness. On Palm Sunday of the Lord's Passion we listen as Jesus was cheered when he rode into Jerusalem on a donkey. Only a few days later the cheering of the crowds would turn into jeering. Jesus would be crucified so we could be forgiven.

Throughout his life on earth, Jesus taught that we are to have forgiving hearts. We are to forgive as God forgives—not once, not twice, but over and over again. We are to be merciful and forgiving—"seventy times seven times," as many times as necessary.

261

Holy Week is a good time to think about how we are living as merciful and forgiving people. But we are to do more than think. We need to ask the Holy Spirit to strengthen and guide us to act as a forgiving people. As followers of Jesus Christ we continue his work of forgiveness throughout our lives.

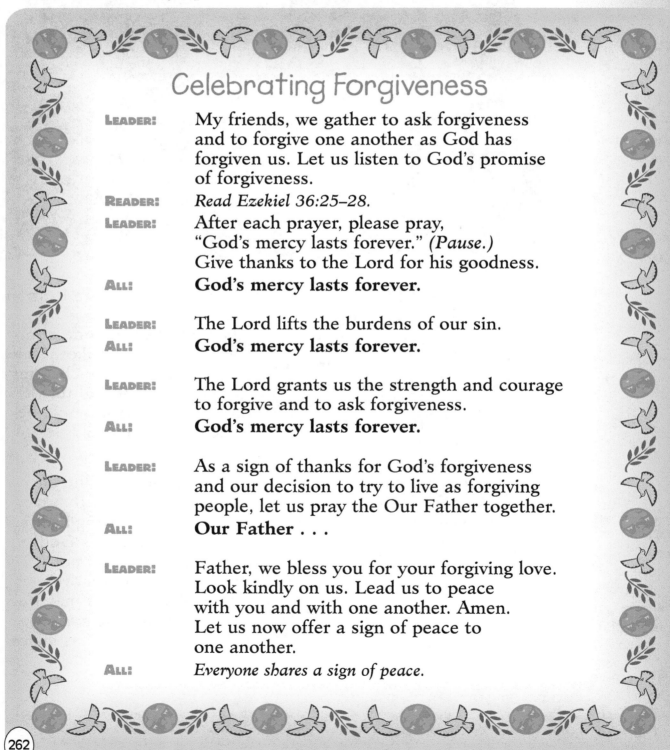

Celebrating Forgiveness

LEADER: My friends, we gather to ask forgiveness and to forgive one another as God has forgiven us. Let us listen to God's promise of forgiveness.

READER: *Read Ezekiel 36:25–28.*

LEADER: After each prayer, please pray, "God's mercy lasts forever." *(Pause.)* Give thanks to the Lord for his goodness.

ALL: **God's mercy lasts forever.**

LEADER: The Lord lifts the burdens of our sin.

ALL: **God's mercy lasts forever.**

LEADER: The Lord grants us the strength and courage to forgive and to ask forgiveness.

ALL: **God's mercy lasts forever.**

LEADER: As a sign of thanks for God's forgiveness and our decision to try to live as forgiving people, let us pray the Our Father together.

ALL: **Our Father . . .**

LEADER: Father, we bless you for your forgiving love. Look kindly on us. Lead us to peace with you and with one another. Amen. Let us now offer a sign of peace to one another.

ALL: *Everyone shares a sign of peace.*

Faith Focus

How does taking part in the liturgy on Holy Thursday help us strengthen our love for God and for one another?

The Word of the Lord

These are the Scripture readings for the Evening Mass of the Lord's Supper on Holy Thursday. Choose one reading. Read and discuss it with your family.

Reading I
    Exodus 12:1–8, 11–14

Reading II
    1 Corinthians 11:23–26

Gospel
    John 13:1–15

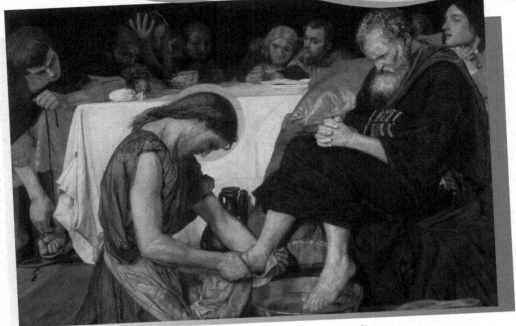

Christ Washing Peter's Feet.
Ford Madox Brown (1821–1893), English painter.

Ancient water jug found during excavations in Jerusalem

Love One Another

There is a saying that goes, "You can't judge a book by its cover." In other words, you cannot know what the book is really about until you read it. The same might be said about people. We really cannot know someone simply by looking at them. We need to listen to them and "see" them in action.

The last three days of Holy Week are called the Triduum, a word that means "a period of three days." The Church's celebration of the Triduum includes the celebration of the Evening Mass of the Lord's Supper on Holy Thursday, the celebration of the Lord's Passion on Good Friday, and the Easter Vigil on Holy Saturday night and the liturgy on Easter Sunday. The Triduum ends with the celebration of Evening Prayer on Easter Sunday evening.

On Holy Thursday, after we listen to the story of the Last Supper proclaimed to us, the priest wraps a cloth around his waist. Kneeling before twelve members of the assembly, he washes and dries their feet. This reminds us that we are to do what Jesus did. Each day we are "to wash one another's feet." We are to look for the opportunity to be kind and generous. We are to treat everyone fairly and respectfully.

After washing the disciples' feet, Jesus returned to the table and shared the Last Supper with them. He took bread and said, "This is my body." Then he took the cup of wine and said, "This is the cup of my blood." We remember Jesus' greatest act of love for us.

We share in the memorial of the sacrifice of his life for our salvation.

The words and actions of our lives, as those of Jesus' life did, are to show our love for God and for one another. We are to live as Christians as well as call ourselves Christians.

Greater Love Than This...

Jesus tells us to love one another unselfishly. Act out and discuss this short play. Do you think there are many people today who would act like the two brothers? Why or why not?

NARRATOR: *Once upon a time, two brothers farmed together. They divided everything down the middle. But one day this changed.*

UNMARRIED BROTHER: My brother is married and has children. He should have more than half of the wheat crop.

MARRIED BROTHER: My brother is not married. He will have no one to take care of him in his old age. He should have more than half of the wheat crop.

NARRATOR: *So in the night of the new moon, the brother who was not married secretly carried sacks of wheat into his married brother's granary. The married brother did the same for his unmarried brother! This went on night after night.*

UNMARRIED BROTHER: Hmmmm. My granary has the same amount of wheat.

MARRIED BROTHER: Hmmmm. My granary has the same amount of wheat.

NARRATOR: *One dark night the brothers ran into each other. They dropped their sacks of wheat. They paused. They understood. They hugged each other. They laughed for joy.*

The place where they met is a holy place. For where love is, there is God.

BASED ON A HASSIDIC TALE

Faith Focus

Why is the cross the central symbol for Christians?

The Word of the Lord

These are the Scripture readings for Good Friday. Choose one reading. Read and discuss it with your family.

Reading I
Isaiah 52:13–53:12

Reading II
Hebrews 4:14–16, 5:7–9

Gospel
John 18:1–19:42

Behold the Wood of the Cross

We are surrounded by symbols. A symbol is an object or action that has a special meaning for us. For example, the flag of our nation is a symbol of the values on which our nation is built. It represents the people who have built and are building our nation, especially those who have given their lives for us. What other symbols are important to you?

The cross, or crucifix, is the central symbol of Christianity. On Good Friday, Catholics around the world gather and pray:

We adore your Cross,
O Lord,
we praise and glorify your
holy Resurrection,
for behold, because of
the wood of a tree
joy has come to the
whole world.

Woodcarving by Carl Bindhammer, contemporary American artist

Dressed in red vestments, the ministers silently enter the church. When they reach the altar steps, they lie facedown for a moment of reflection. Rising, they go to their places and join us in listening to the retelling of the story of God's promise of salvation and its fulfillment in Jesus Christ.

After the Liturgy of the Word concludes, the deacon or priest enters the church and walks through the assembly. Holding the crucifix up high, he sings aloud three times, "Behold the wood of the Cross, on which hung the salvation of the world." Each time we respond, "Come, let us adore."

Everyone in the assembly then approaches the cross and reverences it as the choir sings an appropriate song.

Every time we enter our parish church, the cross reminds us of God's love for us. We remember Jesus' own description of his approaching death:

"The hour has come for the Son of Man to be glorified. Amen, amen, I say to you, unless a grain of wheat falls to the ground and dies, it remains just a grain of wheat; but if it dies, it produces much fruit."

JOHN 12:23–24

The cross stands for the life-giving sacrifice of Jesus. It reminds us of the love of Jesus for his Father and for all people. It stands for the life that we who have been baptized into the death-Resurrection of Christ are called to live.

The Right Choice

Make a list of a few of the many choices you have made or might be asked to make each day because of your love for God and others. Rate each choice as 1, easy; 2, not so easy; or 3, really difficult.

Choice   Rating

_____   _____

_____   _____

_____   _____

_____   _____

_____   _____

Circle your most difficult choice and pray to the Holy Spirit for the gift of courage to make that choice.

Faith Focus

Why is Easter the most important season of the Church's year?

The Word of the Lord

These are the Gospel readings for Easter Sunday. Choose this year's reading. Read and discuss it with your family.

Year A
    John 20:1–9
        or
    Matthew 28:1–10
        or
    Luke 24:13–35

Year B
    John 20:1–9
        or
    Mark 16:1–8
        or
    Luke 24:13–35

Year C
    John 20:1–9
        or
    Luke 24:1–12
        or
    Luke 24:13–35

This Is the Day

There is something special about the farm when crops begin to grow and fill the field. The air is filled with new scents as the smell of winter dirt is transformed into the fresh aroma of new, green life. What signs of spring and new life fill the places where you live and play?

Signs of the new life we have in Christ fill our churches during Easter. At the Easter Vigil the newly lighted Easter candle stands tall and shines in the darkness. Standing and holding lighted candles that flood the church with light, the worshiping assembly listens as the Church proclaims:

Exult, let them exult, the hosts of heaven, . . . sound aloud our mighty King's triumph!

Das Lamb. Paul Klee (1879–1940), Swiss expressionist painter. The New Testament uses the title *Lamb of God* for Christ.

Everyone rejoices. Easter is the Church's season of new life. On Easter Sunday the Church around the world breaks into joyful song and sings, "This is the day the Lord has made; let us be glad and rejoice in it" (Easter Proclamation).

We fill our homes and lives with signs of joy and new life. Flowers and candles decorate our homes. Special foods, such as Easter breads and colored eggs, remind us that this is a life-giving feast. Throughout this day and for fifty days afterward, our celebration of Easter continues. We sing aloud and in the quiet of our hearts, "Alleluia! Alleluia! Alleluia!"

Alleluia! Christ Is Risen

Create a design for an Easter banner in this space. Then, using your design, work with your family to create a banner and hang it in your home.

Faith Focus

How does the story of Saint Thomas the Apostle help us live our Baptism?

The Word of the Lord

This is the Gospel reading for the Second Sunday of Easter. Read and discuss it with your family.

John 20:19–31

What You See

One of the Easter symbols is the Paschal, or Easter, candle. It is lighted at the Easter Vigil and throughout the Easter season. After Pentecost it is used to symbolize Resurrection at baptisms and funerals.

Doubting Thomas? Faithful Thomas?

Eyewitness reportings of events are the most believable. When our friends describe with enthusiasm and in detail things or events they have seen, we become part of their story. It is almost as if we were there. What is an event that you have witnessed and told your friends about?

All four of the Evangelists tell about the witnesses who first learned about Jesus' Resurrection. Mary Magdalene, Mary the mother of James and John, and Salome were the first to come to the empty tomb. Only after hearing the women describe what they had seen did Saint Peter and the other disciples go to the tomb and witness the empty tomb for themselves.

Later the Risen Lord appeared to the disciples. Saint Thomas the Apostle was not present with the others. Because he at first so strongly refused to believe in the Resurrection, people who refuse to believe what others know to be true are called "doubting Thomas."

Stained-glass window of "Doubting Thomas" from the Franciscan Chapel in Jerusalem. According to tradition, the chapel is at the site where the Last Supper took place.

Thomas did not remain a doubter; he too became a strong believer in the Risen Jesus. When the Risen Lord appeared a second time, Thomas loudly and clearly professed his faith. He said, "My Lord and my God!"

Our Baptism began our life in the Risen Lord. The Holy Spirit whom we received at Baptism invites us to live our faith. We proclaim it loudly and clearly in our words and actions.

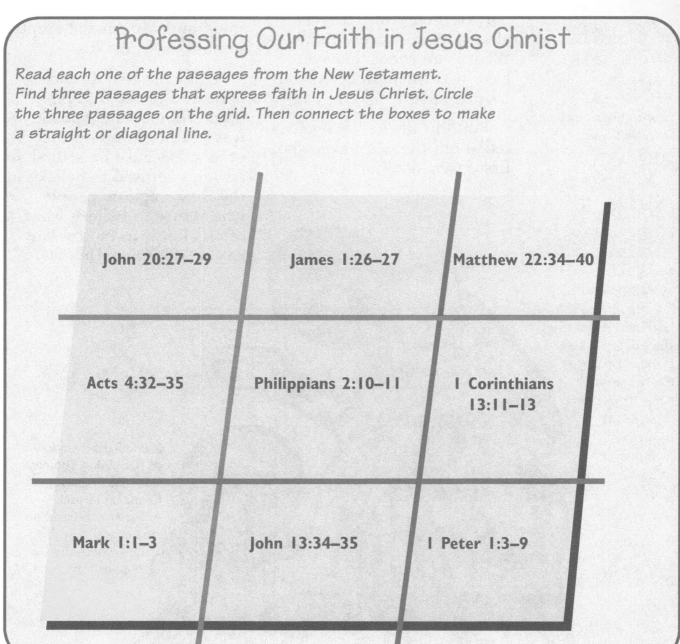

Professing Our Faith in Jesus Christ

Read each one of the passages from the New Testament. Find three passages that express faith in Jesus Christ. Circle the three passages on the grid. Then connect the boxes to make a straight or diagonal line.

John 20:27–29	James 1:26–27	Matthew 22:34–40
Acts 4:32–35	Philippians 2:10–11	I Corinthians 13:11–13
Mark 1:1–3	John 13:34–35	I Peter 1:3–9

Road to Emmaus. The journey from Jerusalem to Emmaus is about seven miles.

Faith Focus

What happened when the Risen Jesus blessed, broke, and shared bread with the two disciples he traveled with to Emmaus?

The Word of the Lord

These are the Gospel readings for the Third Sunday of Easter. Choose this year's reading. Read and discuss it with your family.

Year A
   Luke 24:13–35

Year B
   Luke 24:35–48

Year C
   John 21:1–19 or
   John 21:1–14

The Road to Emmaus

Good news is great to receive. When we receive it, we just cannot help sharing it. When was the last time you received good news? How did you feel? Did you tell anyone else?

The Gospel according to Luke tells us about two disciples who had not yet heard the good news of Jesus' Resurrection. They were puzzled by reports that Jesus had been raised from the dead and he had been seen by many. As they were walking from Jerusalem to Emmaus, they were joined by a "stranger." The stranger was the Risen Jesus, but they did not recognize him.

The two disciples started telling the stranger about Jesus. The Risen Jesus began explaining the Scriptures, which they knew so well, to help them understand everything that had happened.

Finally, as the sun began to set, they were approaching Emmaus, the village where the disciples lived. Amazed and interested in what the "stranger" was telling them, they invited the Risen Jesus to stay with them. While they were eating, Jesus took bread, blessed, and broke it. Then he shared it with them. At that moment the disciples suddenly recognized the stranger to be the Risen Jesus. Jesus immediately disappeared, and the disciples hurried back to Jerusalem to tell the other disciples the good news of what had happened to them (see Luke 24:13–33).

Each week at Mass we listen to the Scriptures and share in the Eucharist, the bread and wine that have become the Body and Blood of Christ. Fed by the word of God and the Eucharist, we are sent forth into our homes, neighborhoods, and schools. We tell others about Jesus and the good news of God's love for us.

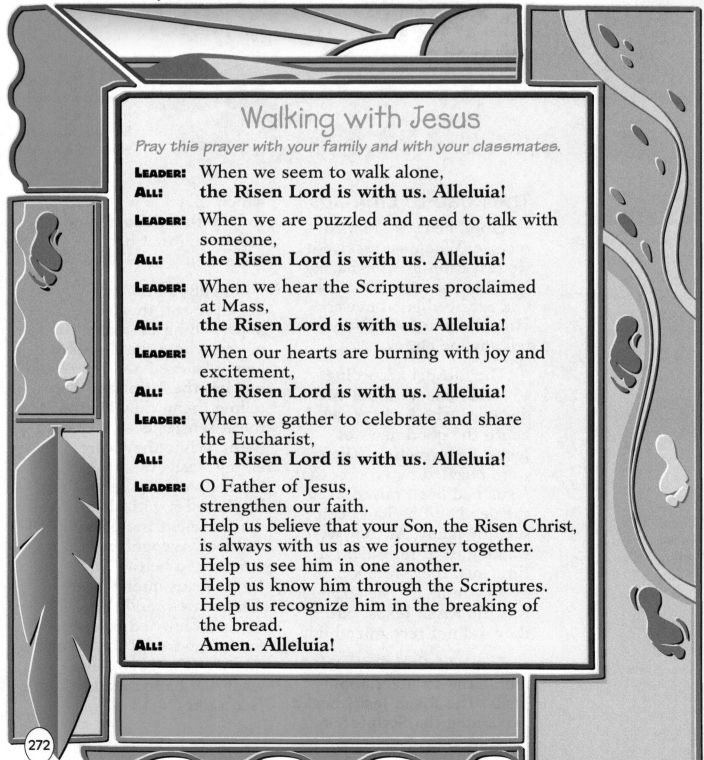

Walking with Jesus

Pray this prayer with your family and with your classmates.

LEADER: When we seem to walk alone,
ALL: the Risen Lord is with us. Alleluia!

LEADER: When we are puzzled and need to talk with someone,
ALL: the Risen Lord is with us. Alleluia!

LEADER: When we hear the Scriptures proclaimed at Mass,
ALL: the Risen Lord is with us. Alleluia!

LEADER: When our hearts are burning with joy and excitement,
ALL: the Risen Lord is with us. Alleluia!

LEADER: When we gather to celebrate and share the Eucharist,
ALL: the Risen Lord is with us. Alleluia!

LEADER: O Father of Jesus,
strengthen our faith.
Help us believe that your Son, the Risen Christ,
is always with us as we journey together.
Help us see him in one another.
Help us know him through the Scriptures.
Help us recognize him in the breaking of the bread.
ALL: Amen. Alleluia!

The Good Shepherd

Faith Focus

How does the image of the Good Shepherd help us understand our relationship to Jesus?

The Word of the Lord

These are the Gospel readings for the Fourth Sunday of Easter. Choose this year's reading. Read and discuss it with your family.

Year A
   John 10:1–10

Year B
   John 10:11–18

Year C
   John 10:27–30

What You See

The priest wears white vestments during the Easter season. White is a symbol of joy and life. We rejoice in Jesus' Resurrection.

Teams have coaches. Schools have principals. Governors are the leaders of our states, and the president is the leader of our country. Good leaders are important. They remind us of the principles and goals of the groups we belong to. Think of a leader you admire. What leadership qualities does this person have?

In the Old Testament the image of a shepherd is often used to describe the leader of God's people. Today we call our bishops the shepherds of the Church.

In the Scriptures the word *shepherd* is also used for God. God is the true shepherd of his people. Jesus also uses this image

Shepherd tending flock near Bethlehem

to describe his relationship to us. He said:

"I am the good shepherd, and I know mine and mine know me, just as the Father knows me and I know the Father; and I will lay down my life for the sheep."

JOHN 10:14–15

Fifteenth-century mosaic of the Good Shepherd

Remembering that Jesus sacrificed his life for them and all people, the early Church used the image of the Good Shepherd to express their faith in Jesus Christ. Jesus is the Good Shepherd who gave his life for us. Through the gifts of faith and Baptism, we choose Jesus to be our shepherd. Through him we share in the life and love of God.

Design a mosaic that shows Jesus is the Good Shepherd.

We Are His People

America's first mission (1565), Saint Augustine, Florida

Singing Psalm 118 during Easter helps us remember that in Baptism we share in the gift of new life God has given us. We sing:

I shall not die, but live, and declare the works of the Lord.

RESPONSORIAL PSALM, EASTER SUNDAY

To help us remember that Jesus is the center of our lives, Saint Peter the Apostle used the image of a cornerstone. He wrote:

Come to him, a living stone. . . . [L]et yourselves be built into a spiritual house to be a holy priesthood to offer spiritual sacrifices acceptable to God through Jesus Christ. For it says in scripture:

"Behold, I am laying a stone in Zion, a cornerstone, chosen and precious."

1 PETER 2:4–6

Faith Focus

How can we remember that Jesus is the center of the lives of all who have been baptized?

The Word of the Lord

These are the Gospel readings for the Fifth Sunday of Easter. Choose this year's reading. Read and discuss it with your family.

Year A
John 14:1–12

Year B
John 15:1–8

Year C
John 13:31–35

Remembering Jesus

Each family celebrates its memories in different ways. Many families collect photos or home videos. Other families have parties and invite family members and friends to share food and memories.

The Church gathers and shares her memories of the Risen Jesus in many ways. During the Easter season we remember that "We proclaim your Death, O Lord, and profess your Resurrection, until you come again." He is always at the center of all our celebrations.

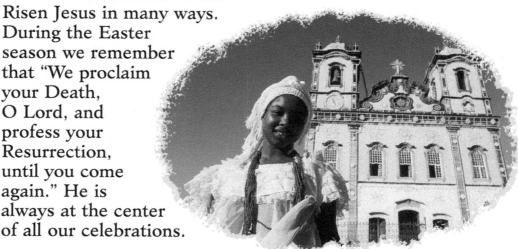

Our Lord of Good Ending Church in Salvador, Brazil

A cornerstone of a building is the stone around which all other stones are built. Christ is the center of the Church. The lives of all who have been baptized are built around and supported by him.

Keeping Jesus at the Center of Our Lives

Saint Paul described Jesus as the cornerstone of the Church. The New Testament has many other images for Jesus. Look up each Gospel passage and name the image it uses for Jesus.

John 6:48 _____

John 8:12 _____

John 10:7 _____

John 15:5 _____

Which image helps you remember that Jesus is the center of your life? How does it help you?

_____

_____

_____

_____

_____

_____

_____

Faith Focus

What actions of Saint Peter and the other Apostles helped people become followers of Jesus?

The Word of the Lord

These are the Gospel readings for the Sixth Sunday of Easter. Choose this year's reading. Read and discuss it with your family.

Year A
    John 14:15–21

Year B
    John 15:9–17

Year C
    John 14:23–29

Proclaiming the Good News

You have probably heard the saying, "Actions speak louder than words." What does this saying mean to you?

There are actions that show we are living as Christians. There are also actions that show we are not living as Christians. Jesus invites us to act as he did. He told his disciples to reach out to heal and forgive others. He told them to go out into the whole world and proclaim the good news of God's love.

From the beginning of the Church, Jesus' disciples have done what he asked. Saint Peter and the other Apostles traveled far from their homes to tell others about Jesus Christ. They preached that Jesus had been crucified and died and was raised from the dead.

They wanted everyone to know that God's salvation was to be found in Jesus Christ (Acts 4:5–12). Saint Peter, Saint Paul, and the other Apostles shared with others this good news of God's love.

They taught that Jesus asks us to make a choice and to change the way we act. Those who changed and were baptized became members of the Church. We are baptized. We are followers of Christ. By our actions others will know that we are Jesus' disciples. By our actions others will come to know God's great love for them.

Living the Good News

Read and respond to each situation. Describe what you would do and say that shows you are a follower of Jesus.

Mateo tells you that his gerbil died. He is so sad that he can hardly talk without crying.

I will _____

_____.

Yi Min is excited. She tells you her grandmother is finally coming from China to visit.

I will _____

_____.

Your little sister is watching TV. It is time for your favorite show to come on.

I will _____

_____.

Think about your day. What can you do or say today that will show you have been baptized and are a follower of Jesus?

I will _____

_____.

Faith Focus

How does the story of Saint Stephen the Deacon help us live our faith in Christ?

The Word of the Lord

These are the Gospel readings for the Seventh Sunday of Easter. Choose this year's reading. Read and discuss it with your family.

Year A
    John 17:1–11

Year B
    John 17:11–19

Year C
    John 17:20–26

The Stoning of Saint Stephen. Paolo Ucello (1397–1475), Italian painter.

Giving Witness to Christ

Sometimes we see or hear or read something that makes us stop and think. It becomes so important to us that we cannot stop telling others about it. Saint Stephen the Deacon could not stop talking about Jesus. His faith in Jesus was so strong that he had to share it.

Some people who listened to Saint Stephen became angry with him because he proclaimed that Jesus was truly God and was the Promised One of whom Moses and the prophets had spoken. They insisted that Stephen stop teaching. When Stephen refused, they decided he had to die. After throwing Stephen in a ditch, they kept hurling stones at him until he died.

Since the first days of the Church, Christians have honored Saint Stephen the Deacon as a martyr. The Greek word *martyr* means "witness." Saint Stephen gave witness to his faith in Jesus Christ to the point of dying for his faith.

Saint Paul teaches that all who are baptized into Christ's death and Resurrection are given the grace and vocation to witness to Christ (see Ephesians 2:19). While most Christians will never be faced with dying for their faith as Stephen did, all the baptized must give witness to our faith in Christ.

Witness Awards

Think of a courageous, loving follower of Jesus whom you admire. In this space, design a medallion honoring that person as a witness to his or her faith in the Risen Jesus.

The Gift of the Holy Spirit

When we play a game, we feel team spirit. That spirit gives us the courage and enthusiasm to do our best. When do you feel a spirit that moves you to be courageous or generous or kind?

After the Risen Lord ascended to his Father in heaven, his disciples gathered in a house in Jerusalem. There, on the Jewish feast of Pentecost, a great wind filled the room. Flames, like tongues of fire, settled above them. This was a sign that the Holy Spirit had come to the disciples as Jesus promised. The Holy Spirit filled the disciples with joy and courage.

When Peter preached about Jesus to people who had come to Jerusalem from many countries, each person understood Peter in their own language. Many listened and the Holy Spirit moved them to be baptized.

Each year the Church celebrates Pentecost. On Pentecost we stand and sing: Come, Holy Spirit, fill the hearts of your faithful; and kindle in them the fire of your love.

GOSPEL ALLELUIA, PENTECOST

Christians are temples of the Holy Spirit. The Holy Spirit is so close to us that he lives within us. Each Pentecost we remember that we have received the gift of the Holy Spirit at Baptism. We ask the Holy Spirit to fill us with his gifts to live our Baptism.

Living as Temples of the Holy Spirit

Saint Paul the Apostle names nine signs, or fruits, of living a life guided by the Holy Spirit. Read Galatians 5:22–23 to discover these signs. List them in this space.

_____   _____

_____   _____

_____   _____

_____   _____

_____

Describe a situation in which you have seen one or several of these qualities in someone else or in yourself.

_____

_____

_____

_____

_____

Catholic Prayers and Practices

Sign of the Cross

In the name of the Father,
and of the Son,
and of the Holy Spirit. Amen.

Glory Be

Glory be to the Father
and to the Son
and to the Holy Spirit,
as it was in the beginning
is now, and ever shall be
world without end. Amen.

Lord's Prayer

Our Father, who art in heaven,
hallowed be thy name;
thy kingdom come,
thy will be done
on earth as it is in heaven.
Give us this day our daily bread,
and forgive us our trespasses,
as we forgive those who trespass
against us;
and lead us not into temptation,
but deliver us from evil. Amen.

Prayer to the Holy Spirit

Come, Holy Spirit, fill the hearts
of your faithful.
And kindle in them the
fire of your love.
Send forth your Spirit and
they shall be created.
And you will renew the
face of the earth.

Hail Mary

Hail, Mary, full of grace,
the Lord is with thee.
Blessed art thou among women
and blessed is the fruit of thy
womb, Jesus.
Holy Mary, Mother of God,
pray for us sinners,
now and at the hour of our death.
Amen.

Act of Contrition

My God,
I am sorry for my sins
with all my heart.
In choosing to do wrong
and failing to do good,
I have sinned against you
whom I should love above all things.
I firmly intend, with your help,
to do penance,
to sin no more,
and to avoid whatever leads me to sin.
Our Savior Jesus Christ
suffered and died for us.
In his name, my God, have mercy.

Apostles' Creed

I believe in God,
the Father almighty,
Creator of heaven and earth,
and in Jesus Christ,
    his only Son, our Lord,

*(At the words that follow, up to and
including the Virgin Mary, all bow.)*

who was conceived by the Holy Spirit,
born of the Virgin Mary,
suffered under Pontius Pilate,
was crucified, died and was buried;
he descended into hell;
on the third day he rose again
    from the dead;
he ascended into heaven,
and is seated at the right hand
    of God the Father almighty;
from there he will come to judge
    the living and the dead.

I believe in the Holy Spirit,
the holy catholic Church,
the communion of saints,
the forgiveness of sins,
the resurrection of the body,
and life everlasting. Amen.

Nicene Creed

I believe in one God,
the Father almighty,
maker of heaven and earth,
of all things visible and invisible.

I believe in one Lord Jesus Christ,
the Only Begotten Son of God,
born of the Father before all ages.
God from God, Light from Light,
true God from true God,

begotten, not made, consubstantial
    with the Father;
through him all things were made.
For us men and for our salvation
he came down from heaven,

*(At the words that follow, up to and
including and became man, all bow.)*

and by the Holy Spirit
    was incarnate of the Virgin Mary,
and became man.

For our sake he was crucified under
    Pontius Pilate,
he suffered death and was buried,
and rose again on the third day
in accordance with the Scriptures.
He ascended into heaven
and is seated at the right hand
    of the Father.
He will come again in glory
to judge the living and the dead
and his kingdom will have no end.

I believe in the Holy Spirit, the Lord,
    the giver of life,
who proceeds from the Father and the Son,
who with the Father and the Son
    is adored and glorified,
who has spoken through the prophets.

I believe in one, holy, catholic and
    apostolic Church.
I confess one Baptism
    for the forgiveness of sins
and I look forward to the resurrection
    of the dead
and the life of the world to come.
Amen.

Morning Prayer

Dear God,
as I begin this day,
keep me in your love and care.
Help me to live as your child today.
Bless me, my family, and my friends
   in all we do.
Keep us all close to you. Amen.

Evening Prayer

Dear God,
I thank you for today.
Keep me safe throughout the night.
Thank you for all the good I did today.
I am sorry for what I have chosen
   to do wrong.
Bless my family and friends. Amen.

Grace Before Meals

Bless us, O Lord,
   and these thy gifts,
which we are about to receive
   from thy bounty,
through Christ our Lord.
Amen.

Grace After Meals

We give thee thanks, for all
   thy benefits, almighty God,
who lives and reigns forever.
Amen.

A Vocation Prayer

God, I know you will call me
for special work in my life.
Help me follow Jesus each day
and be ready to answer your call.

Act of Faith

O my God, I firmly believe that you are
one God in three divine Persons, Father,
Son, and Holy Spirit; I believe that your
divine Son became man and died for our
sins, and that he will come to judge the
living and the dead. Amen.

Act of Hope

O my God, relying on your infinite
goodness and promises, I hope to obtain
pardon of my sins, the help of your grace,
and life everlasting, through the merits of
Jesus Christ, my Lord and Redeemer.
Amen.

Act of Love

O my God, I love you above all things,
with my whole heart and soul, because
you are all good and worthy of all my love.
I love my neighbor as myself for the love
of you. I forgive all who have injured me
and I ask pardon of all whom I have
injured. Amen.

The Divine Praises

Blessed be God.
Blessed be his holy name.
Blessed be Jesus Christ, true God and
true man.
Blessed be the name of Jesus.
Blessed be his most Sacred Heart.
Blessed be his most precious Blood.
Blessed be Jesus in the most holy
Sacrament of the altar.
Blessed be the Holy Spirit, the Paraclete.
Blessed be the great Mother of God,
Mary most holy.
Blessed be her holy and Immaculate
Conception.
Blessed be her glorious Assumption.
Blessed be the name of Mary, Virgin and
Mother.
Blessed be Saint Joseph, her most chaste
spouse.
Blessed be God in his angels and in his
saints.

Prayer of Saint Francis

Lord, make me an instrument of your
peace:
where there is hatred, let me sow love;
where there is injury, pardon;
where there is doubt, faith;
where there is despair, hope;
where there is darkness, light;
where there is sadness, joy.

O divine Master, grant that
I may not so much seek
to be consoled as to console,
to be understood as to understand,
to be loved as to love.
For it is in giving that we receive,
it is in pardoning that we are pardoned,
it is in dying that we are born to
eternal life.
Amen.

The Angelus

Leader: The Angel of the Lord declared
unto Mary,
Response: And she conceived of the
Holy Spirit.
All: Hail Mary . . .

Leader: Behold the handmaid of the Lord,
Response: Be it done unto me according to
your Word.
All: Hail Mary . . .

Leader: And the Word was made flesh
Response: And dwelt among us.
All: Hail Mary . . .

Leader: Pray for us, O holy Mother
of God,
Response: That we may be made worthy of the
promises of Christ.

Leader: Let us pray.
Pour forth, we beseech you,
O Lord, your grace into our hearts:
that we, to whom the Incarnation
of Christ your Son was made known
by the message of an Angel, may by
his Passion and Cross be brought
to the glory of his Resurrection.
Through the same Christ our Lord.
All: Amen.

The Great Commandment

"You shall love the Lord,
your God, with all your
heart, with all your soul,
and with all your mind. . . .
You shall love your neighbor as yourself."

MATTHEW 22:37, 39

The New Commandment

[Jesus said:] "I give you a new
commandment: love one another.
As I have loved you, so you also should
love one another. This is how all will
know that you are my disciples,
if you have love for one another."

JOHN 13:34–35

The Ten Commandments

1. I am the LORD your God: you shall
   not have strange gods before me.
2. You shall not take the name of the
   LORD your God in vain.
3. Remember to keep holy the
   LORD's Day.
4. Honor your father and your mother.
5. You shall not kill.
6. You shall not commit adultery.
7. You shall not steal.
8. You shall not bear false witness
   against your neighbor.
9. You shall not covet your neighbor's wife.
10. You shall not covet your neighbor's
    goods.

The Beatitudes

"Blessed are the poor in spirit,
  for theirs is the kingdom of heaven.
Blessed are they who mourn,
  for they will be comforted.
Blessed are the meek,
  for they will inherit the land.
Blessed are they who hunger
    and thirst for righteousness,
  for they will be satisfied.
Blessed are the merciful,
  for they will be shown mercy.
Blessed are the clean of heart,
  for they will see God.
Blessed are the peacemakers,
  for they will be called children of God.
Blessed are they who are persecuted
    for the sake of righteousness,
  for theirs is the kingdom of heaven.

Blessed are you when they insult you
and persecute you and utter every kind
of evil against you [falsely] because of me.
Rejoice and be glad, for your reward will
be great in heaven."

MATTHEW 5:3–12

Corporal Works of Mercy

Feed people who are hungry.
Give drink to people who are thirsty.
Clothe people who need clothes.
Visit prisoners.
Shelter people who are homeless.
Visit people who are sick.
Bury people who have died.

Spiritual Works of Mercy

Help people who sin.
Teach people who are ignorant.
Give advice to people
    who have doubts.
Comfort people who suffer.
Be patient with other people.
Forgive people who hurt you.
Pray for people who are alive and for
    those who have died.

Gifts of the Holy Spirit

Wisdom
Understanding
Right judgment (Counsel)
Courage (Fortitude)
Knowledge
Reverence (Piety)
Wonder and awe (Fear of the Lord)

Cardinal Virtues

Prudence
Justice
Fortitude
Temperance

Precepts of the Church

1. Participate in Mass on Sundays and holy days of obligation and rest from unnecessary work.

2. Confess sins at least once a year.

3. Receive Holy Communion at least during the Easter season.

4. Observe the prescribed days of fasting and abstinence.

5. Provide for the material needs of the Church, each according to one's abilities.

Basic Principles of the Church's Teaching on Social Justice

The Church's teaching on social justice guides us in living lives of holiness and building a just society. These principles are:

1. All human life is sacred. The basic equality of all people flows from their dignity as human persons and the rights that flow from that dignity.

2. The human person is the principle, the object, and the subject of every social group.

3. The human person has been created by God to belong to and to participate in a family and other social communities.

4. Respect for the rights of people flows from their dignity as persons. Society and all social organizations must promote virtue and protect human life and human rights and guarantee the conditions that promote the exercise of freedom.

5. Political communities and public authority are based on human nature. They belong to an order established by God.

6. All human authority must be used for the common good of society.

7. The common good of society consists of respect for and promotion of the fundamental rights of the human person; the just development of material and spiritual goods of society; and the peace and safety of all people.

8. We need to work to eliminate the sinful inequalities that exist between peoples and for the improvement of the living conditions of people. The needs of the poor and vulnerable have a priority.

9. We are one human and global family. We are to share our spiritual blessings, even more than our material blessings.

Based on the *Catechism of the Catholic Church*

Rosary

Catholics pray the Rosary to honor Mary and remember the important events in the lives of Jesus and Mary. There are twenty mysteries of the Rosary. Follow the steps from 1 to 5.

3. Think of the first mystery. Pray an Our Father, 10 Hail Marys, and the Glory Be.

5. Pray the Hail, Holy Queen prayer. Make the Sign of the Cross.

2. Pray an Our Father, 3 Hail Marys, and the Glory Be.

4. Repeat step 3 for each of the next 4 mysteries.

1. Make the Sign of the Cross and pray the Apostles' Creed.

Joyful Mysteries

1. The Annunciation
2. The Visitation
3. The Nativity
4. The Presentation in the Temple
5. The Finding of the Child Jesus After Three Days in the Temple

Luminous Mysteries

1. The Baptism at the Jordan
2. The Miracle at Cana
3. The Proclamation of the Kingdom and the Call to Conversion
4. The Transfiguration
5. The Institution of the Eucharist

Sorrowful Mysteries

1. The Agony in the Garden
2. The Scourging at the Pillar
3. The Crowning with Thorns
4. The Carrying of the Cross
5. The Crucifixion and Death

Glorious Mysteries

1. The Resurrection
2. The Ascension
3. The Descent of the Holy Spirit at Pentecost
4. The Assumption of Mary
5. The Crowning of the Blessed Virgin as Queen of Heaven and Earth

Hail, Holy Queen

Hail, holy Queen, Mother of mercy:
Hail, our life, our sweetness and our hope.
To you do we cry, poor banished
    children of Eve.
To you do we send up our sighs,
mourning and weeping
    in this valley of tears.
Turn then, most gracious advocate,
your eyes of mercy toward us;
and after this our exile
show unto us the blessed fruit
    of your womb, Jesus.
O clement, O loving, O sweet Virgin Mary.

Stations of the Cross

1. Jesus is condemned to death.

2. Jesus accepts his cross.

3. Jesus falls the first time.

4. Jesus meets his mother.

5. Simon helps Jesus carry the cross.

6. Veronica wipes the face of Jesus.

7. Jesus falls the second time.

8. Jesus meets the women.

9. Jesus falls the third time.

10. Jesus is stripped of his clothes.

11. Jesus is nailed to the cross.

12. Jesus dies on the cross.

13. Jesus is taken down from the cross.

14. Jesus is buried in the tomb.

Some parishes conclude the Stations by reflecting on the Resurrection of Jesus.

Signs and Symbols of the Catholic Church

From its beginning the Church used signs and symbols to help us profess our faith. These symbols unite us. They help us understand what Catholics believe.

Cross

The cross is one of the most widely used symbols of our faith. It reminds us that Jesus died on the cross and was raised from the dead. A crucifix is a cross with Jesus' body fixed to it.

Alpha and Omega

Alpha and Omega are the first and last letters of the Greek alphabet. They remind us that Jesus is the beginning and end of everything that is.

Chi-Rho

The Chi-Rho is a symbol for Christ. It comes from the first two letters of the Greek word for Christ.

The Good Shepherd

Jesus is often represented as the Good Shepherd who leads and cares for his sheep. The sheep symbolize those who follow Christ.

Paschal Candle

The Paschal candle, also called the Easter candle, is a symbol of the Risen Christ who is the Light of the world.

The Seven Sacraments

Jesus gave the Church the seven sacraments. The sacraments are the main liturgical signs of the Church. They make the Paschal Mystery of Jesus, who is always the main celebrant of each sacrament, present to us. They make us sharers in the saving work of Christ and in the life of the Holy Trinity.

Sacraments of Initiation

Baptism

Through Baptism we are joined to Christ and become members of the Body of Christ, the Church. We are reborn as adopted children of God the Father and receive the gift of the Holy Spirit. Original sin and all personal sins are forgiven.

Confirmation

Confirmation completes Baptism. In this sacrament the gift of the Holy Spirit strengthens us to live our Baptism.

Eucharist

Sharing in the Eucharist joins us most fully to Christ and to the Church. We share in the one sacrifice of Christ. The bread and wine become the Body and Blood of Christ through the power of the Holy Spirit and the words of the priest. We receive the Body and Blood of Christ.

Sacraments of Healing

Penance and Reconciliation

Through the ministry of the priest we receive forgiveness of sins committed after our Baptism. We need to confess all mortal sins.

Anointing of the Sick

Anointing of the Sick strengthens our faith and trust in God when we are seriously ill, dying, or weak because of old age.

Sacraments at the Service of Communion

Holy Orders

Through Holy Orders a baptized man is consecrated to serve the whole Church as a bishop, priest, or deacon in the name of Christ. Bishops, who are the successors of the Apostles, receive this sacrament most fully. They are consecrated to teach the Gospel, to lead the Church in the worship of God, and to guide the Church to live holy lives. Bishops are helped by priests, their coworkers, and by deacons in their work.

Matrimony

Matrimony unites a baptized man and a baptized woman in a lifelong bond of faithful love to always honor each other and to accept the gift of children from God. In this sacrament the married couple is consecrated to be a sign of Christ's love for the Church.

We Celebrate the Mass

The Introductory Rites

**We remember that we are the community
of the Church. We prepare to listen to the word of God
and to celebrate the Eucharist.**

The Entrance

We stand as the priest, deacon, and other ministers enter the assembly. We sing a gathering song. The priest and deacon kiss the altar. The priest then goes to the chair where he presides over the celebration.

Sign of the Cross and Greeting

The priest leads us in praying the Sign of the Cross. The priest greets us, and we say,

"And with your spirit."

The Penitential Act

We admit our wrongdoings.
We bless God for his mercy.

The Gloria

We praise God for all the good he has done for us.

The Collect

The priest leads us in praying the Collect. We respond, **"Amen."**

The Liturgy of the Word

**God speaks to us today.
We listen and respond to God's word.**

The First Reading from the Bible

We sit and listen as the reader reads from the Old Testament or from the Acts of the Apostles. The reader concludes, "The word of the Lord." We respond,

"Thanks be to God."

The Responsorial Psalm

The song leader leads us in singing a psalm.

The Second Reading from the Bible

The reader reads from the New Testament, but not from the four Gospels. The reader concludes, "The word of the Lord." We respond,

"Thanks be to God."

Acclamation

We stand to honor Christ present with us in the Gospel. The song leader leads us in singing **"Alleluia, Alleluia, Alleluia"** or another chant during Lent.

The Gospel

The deacon or priest proclaims, "A reading from the holy Gospel according to (name of Gospel writer)." We respond,

"Glory to you, Lord."

He proclaims the Gospel. At the end, he says, "The Gospel of the Lord." We respond,

"Praise to you, Lord Jesus Christ."

The Homily

We sit. The priest or deacon preaches the homily. He helps the whole community understand the word of God spoken to us in the readings.

The Profession of Faith

We stand and profess our faith.
We pray the Nicene Creed together.

The Prayer of the Faithful

The priest leads us in praying for our Church and its leaders, for our country and its leaders, for ourselves and others, for the sick and those who have died. We can respond to each prayer in several ways. One way we respond is,

"Lord, hear our prayer."

The Liturgy of the Eucharist
We join with Jesus and the Holy Spirit
to give thanks and praise to God the Father.

The Preparation of the Gifts

We sit as the altar table is prepared and the collection is taken up. We share our blessings with the community of the Church and especially with those in need. The song leader may lead us in singing a song. The gifts of bread and wine are brought to the altar.

The priest lifts up the bread and blesses God for all our gifts. He prays, "Blessed are you, Lord God of all creation, . . ."
We respond,
> **"Blessed be God for ever."**

The priest lifts up the cup of wine and prays, "Blessed are you, Lord God of all creation, . . ." We respond,
> **"Blessed be God for ever."**

The priest invites us,
> "Pray, brethren (brothers and sisters),
> that my sacrifice and yours may be acceptable
> to God, the almighty Father."

We stand and respond,
> **"May the Lord accept the sacrifice at your hands for the praise and glory of his name, for our good and the good of all his holy Church."**

The Prayer over the Offerings

The priest leads us in praying the Prayer over the Offerings. We respond, **"Amen."**

Preface

The priest invites us to join in praying the Church's great prayer of praise and thanksgiving to God the Father.

Priest:	"The Lord be with you."
Assembly:	**"And with your spirit."**
Priest:	"Lift up your hearts."
Assembly:	**"We lift them up to the Lord."**
Priest:	"Let us give thanks to the Lord our God."
Assembly:	**"It is right and just."**

After the priest sings or prays aloud the preface, we join in acclaiming,
> **"Holy, Holy, Holy Lord God of hosts.**
> **Heaven and earth are full of**
> **your glory.**
> **Hosanna in the highest.**
> **Blessed is he who comes in**
> **the name of the Lord.**
> **Hosanna in the highest."**

The Eucharistic Prayer

The priest leads the assembly in praying the Eucharistic Prayer. We call upon the Holy Spirit to make our gifts of bread and wine holy and that they become the Body and Blood of Jesus. We recall what happened at the Last Supper. The bread and wine become the Body and Blood of the Lord. Jesus is truly and really present under the appearances of bread and wine.

The priest sings or says aloud, "The mystery of faith." We respond using this or another acclamation used by the Church,
> **"We proclaim your Death, O Lord, and profess your Resurrection until you come again."**

The priest then prays for the Church. He prays for the living and the dead.

Doxology

The priest concludes the praying of the Eucharistic Prayer. He sings or prays aloud,
> "Through him, and with him, and in him, O God, almighty Father, in the unity of the Holy Spirit, all glory and honor is yours, for ever and ever."

We stand and respond, **"Amen."**

The Communion Rite

The Lord's Prayer

We pray the Lord's Prayer together.

The Rite of Peace

The priest invites us to share a sign of peace, saying, "The peace of the Lord be with you always." We respond, **"And with your spirit."** We share a sign of peace.

The Fraction, or the Breaking of the Bread

The priest breaks the host, the consecrated bread. We sing or pray aloud,

**"Lamb of God, you take away
the sins of the world,
   have mercy on us.
Lamb of God, you take away
the sins of the world,
   have mercy on us.
Lamb of God, you take away
the sins of the world,
   grant us peace."**

Communion

The priest raises the host and says aloud,
   "Behold the Lamb of God, behold him
      who takes away the sins of the world.
   Blessed are those called
      to the supper of the Lamb."
We join with him and say,
   **"Lord, I am not worthy that you
   should enter under my roof, but
   only say the word and my soul
   shall be healed."**

The priest receives Communion. Next, the deacon and the extraordinary ministers of Holy Communion and the members of the assembly receive Communion.

The priest, deacon, or extraordinary minister of Holy Communion holds up the host. We bow and the priest, deacon, or extraordinary minister of Holy Communion says, "The Body of Christ." We respond, **"Amen."** We then receive the consecrated host in our hand or on our tongue.

If we are to receive the Blood of Christ, the priest, deacon, or extraordinary minister of Holy Communion holds up the cup containing the consecrated wine. We bow and the priest, deacon, or extraordinary minister of Holy Communion says, "The Blood of Christ." We respond, **"Amen."** We take the cup in our hands and drink from it.

The Prayer after Communion

We stand as the priest invites us to pray, saying, "Let us pray." He prays the Prayer after Communion. We respond, **"Amen."**

The Concluding Rites

**We are sent forth to do good works,
praising and blessing the Lord.**

Greeting

We stand. The priest greets us as
we prepare to leave. He says, "The
Lord be with you." We respond,
"And with your spirit."

Blessing

The priest or deacon may invite us,
"Bow down for the blessing."
The priest blesses us, saying,
"May almighty God bless you, the Father,
and the Son, and the Holy Spirit."
We respond, **"Amen."**

Dismissal of the People

The priest or deacon sends us forth,
using these or similar words,
"Go and announce
the Gospel of the Lord."
We respond,
"Thanks be to God."

We sing a hymn. The priest and the
deacon kiss the altar. The priest, deacon,
and other ministers bow to the altar and
leave in procession.

The Sacrament of Penance and Reconciliation

Individual Rite

Greeting

Scripture Reading

Confession of Sins and Acceptance
of Penance

Act of Contrition

Absolution

Closing Prayer

Communal Rite

Greeting

Scripture Reading

Homily

Examination of Conscience with a litany of
contrition and the Lord's Prayer

Individual Confession and Absolution

Closing Prayer

Glossary

A–B

Abba [page 46]
The name Jesus used for God the Father that reveals the love and trust that exist between Jesus, God the Son, and God the Father.

absolution [page 139]
The forgiveness of sins given by God through the ministry of the priest in the sacrament of Reconciliation.

actual grace [page 174]
The gift of God's presence with us to help us live as children of God and followers of Christ.

Adonai [page 46]
The Hebrew word for "Lord" that the Jewish people use in place of YHWH, the name God revealed for himself to Moses.

Advocate [page 72]
Title or name for the Holy Spirit, which means "one who is at our side," or "one who speaks for us."

almighty [page 46]
Having all power; only God is almighty.

annunciation [page 30]
A word meaning "announcement."

Annunciation [page 30]
The announcement to the Virgin Mary by the angel Gabriel that God had chosen her to be the Mother of Jesus, the Son of God, through the power of the Holy Spirit.

Anointing of the Sick [page 138]
The Sacrament of Healing that strengthens our faith, hope, and love for God when we are seriously ill, weakened by old age, or dying.

Ascension [page 64]
A word meaning "a going up"; the return of the Risen Christ in glory to his Father.

assembly [pages 124, 253]
The community of the Church gathered to celebrate the sacraments and the liturgy.

attributes of God [page 46]
Qualities of God that help us understand the mystery of God.

Baptism [page 106]
The Sacrament of Christian Initiation in which we are first joined to Jesus Christ, become members of the Church, are reborn as God's adopted children, receive the gift of the Holy Spirit, and original sin and our personal sins are forgiven.

Beatitudes [page 166]
The sayings or teachings of Jesus that are found in the Sermon of the Mount and describe both the qualities and the actions of people blessed by God.

bishop [pages 86, 108, 147]
A successor of the Apostles; a priest who has received the fullness of the sacrament of Holy Orders; a member of the order of bishops, or the episcopal college.

breaking of bread [page 130]
A name used for the celebration of the Eucharist.

C–D

catholic letters [page 182]
The seven New Testament letters that bear the names of the Apostles John, Peter, Jude, and James.

chant [page 210]
Plainsong; a simple type of song with only one melody line, using rhythm of the spoken word.

charisms [page 78]
Graces, or gifts, given by the Holy Spirit to build up the Church on earth for the good of all people and the needs of the world.

chastity [page 198]
The virtue that is the good habit of respecting and honoring our sexuality that guides us to share our love with others in appropriate ways.

chrism [page 106]
One of the three oils blessed by the Church to use in the celebration of the liturgy.

christ [page 54]
A Greek word that translates the Hebrew word for *messiah*, which means "anointed one."

Christ [page 54]
A title for Jesus that states that he is the Messiah who God promised to send to save his people.

Church [page 86]
The Body of Christ; the new People of God called together in Christ by the power of the Holy Spirit.

communal prayer [page 218]
Praying with others.

Communion of Saints [page 88]
All the faithful followers of Jesus, both the living and the dead, those on earth, in purgatory, and in heaven.

confession [page 139]
The telling of sins to a priest in the sacrament of Reconciliation.

Confirmation [page 106]
The Sacrament of Christian Initiation that strengthens the graces of Baptism and in which our new life in Christ is sealed by the gift of the Holy Spirit.

conscience [page 158]
The gift of God that is part of every person and that guides us to know and judge what is right and wrong.

consecrate [page 146]
To set aside for a holy purpose.

contrition [page 139]
Sorrow for sins, which includes the desire to make up for the harm our sin has caused.

Covenant [page 190]
The solemn agreement that God entered into with people, promising that he would be their God and they were to be his chosen people.

creed [page 32]
A statement of beliefs; a profession of faith.

Crucifixion [pages 63, 211]
The event of Jesus' saving death on the cross.

deacon [pages 86, 147]
A baptized man who has received the sacrament of Holy Orders; a member of the order of deacons, or the diaconate; a helper of bishops and priests.

divine Revelation [page 14]
God's making known over time the mystery of God and the divine plan of creation and salvation.

disciple [page 226]
A person who learns from and follows the teachings of another person.

E-F-G-H

epistle [page 130]
A type of formal letter found in the New Testament.

eternal [page 46]
Always living, without beginning and without end.

Eucharist [page 122]
The Sacrament of Christian Initiation in which we share in the Paschal Mystery of Christ, we receive the Body and Blood of Christ, and we are joined most fully to Christ and to the Church, the Body of Christ.

evangelist [page 70]
A word meaning "one who announces good news."

Evangelists [page 70]
The writers of the four Gospels in the New Testament—Matthew, Mark, Luke, and John.

evangelization [page 229]
The Church's responsibility to care for and share the Gospel with all people "so that it may enter the hearts of all men and renew the human race."

faith [page 14]
A supernatural gift and power from God inviting us to know and believe in him and our free response to that invitation.

Gospel [page 22]
The Good News of God's love revealed in the life, death, Resurrection, and Ascension of Jesus Christ.

Gospels [page 24]
The first four books of the New Testament that pass on the faith of the Apostles and the early Church about the life, death, Resurrection, Ascension, and teachings of Jesus Christ.

grace [page 174]
The gift of God's life and love that makes us holy and helps us live holy lives.

Holy Orders [page 146]
The Sacrament at the Service of Communion through which a baptized man is consecrated to serve the whole Church as a bishop, priest, or deacon.

Holy Spirit [pages 30, 69–75]
The third Person of the Holy Trinity, sent to us by the Father in the name of his Son, Jesus Christ.

Holy Trinity [page 30]
The central belief of the Christian faith; the mystery of one God in three divine Persons—God the Father, God the Son, God the Holy Spirit.

I-J-K-L

Incarnation [page 55]
From the Latin word meaning "putting on flesh," to have a real body; the Son of God "putting on flesh," or becoming human, while keeping his divinity.

inspiration of the Bible [page 22]
The Holy Spirit guiding the human writers of Sacred Scripture to faithfully and accurately communicate God's word.

Israelites [pages 15, 62]
The Old Testament people to whom God revealed himself and with whom he made the Covenant.

justice [page 198]
The moral, or cardinal, virtue that is the good habit of giving God and all people what is rightfully due to them.

kingdom of God [page 86]
All people and creation living in communion with God at the end of time when the work of Christ will be completed and he will come again in glory.

liturgical year [pages 99, 236–237]
The Church's yearly cycle of seasons and feasts that celebrate the mysteries of Jesus' birth, life, death, and Resurrection.

liturgy [page 98]
The work of the Church, the People of God, of worshiping him through which Christ continues the work of Redemption in, with, and through his Church.

Lord [page 46]
A word that translates the Hebrew word *Adonai,* which the Israelites used for God.

Lord [page 54]
A title for Jesus that states that Jesus is truly God.

Lord's Day [pages 192, 195]
The name Christians give to Sunday, the day of the Lord's Resurrection.

M-N-O

Marks of the Church [page 87]
One, holy, catholic, apostolic; the four signs, or essential qualities, of the Church founded by Jesus.

Mass [page 122]
The main sacramental celebration of the Church at which we gather to listen to God's word and share in the Eucharist.

Matrimony [page 146]
The Sacrament at the Service of Communion that unites a baptized man and a baptized woman in a lifelong bond, or covenant, of faithful love to serve the Church as a sign of Christ's love for the Church.

Messiah [pages 54, 241]
A title that means "Anointed One"; Jesus, the Anointed One of God, the Messiah, the Savior of the world.

miracle [page 38]
An action that goes beyond the laws of nature and invites us to deepen our faith in God.

moral decisions [page 158]
The decisions and choices we make to live as children of God and followers of Jesus Christ.

moral virtues [page 160]
The four virtues of prudence, justice, fortitude, and temperance; they are also called the cardinal virtues.

mortal sin [page 176]
A serious failure in our love and respect for God, our neighbor, creation, and ourselves. Three things are necessary for a sin to be mortal, namely, (1) the thing we do or say must be gravely wrong; (2) we must know it is gravely wrong; (3) we must freely choose it.

Nicene Creed [pages 32, 284]
A creed, or brief statement of the faith of the Church, written in the fourth century.

original sin [page 48]
The sin of Adam and Eve by which they and all people lost the state of original holiness, and death, evil, and suffering entered the world.

P-Q

Paschal Mystery [page 62]
The "passing over" of Jesus from life through death into new and glorious life; the Passion, death, Resurrection, and glorious Ascension of Jesus.

Passover [page 62]
The Jewish feast celebrating the sparing of the Hebrew children from death and the passage of God's people from slavery in Egypt to freedom in the land God promised them.

pastoral administrator [page 149]
A nonordained member of the Church appointed by the bishop of a diocese to be the leader of a parish.

penance [page 139]
Prayer or act of kindness that shows we are truly sorry for our sins.

Pentateuch [page 23]
Word meaning "five containers"; the first five books of the Old Testament.

pentecost [page 114]
A word meaning "fiftieth day."

Pentecost [page 114]
The feast and holy day on which the Church celebrates the coming of the Holy Spirit on the disciples.

personal prayer [page 218]
Praying alone.

priest [page 147]
A baptized man who has received the sacrament of Holy Orders; a member of the order of priests, or the presbyterate; a coworker of the bishops.

Psalms [page 210]
The prayer songs found in the Old Testament Book of Psalms, or the Psalter.

public ministry of Jesus [page 38]
The work that God the Father sent Jesus, the Son of God, to do on earth with the help of the Holy Spirit.

R-S

Reconciliation [page 138]
The Sacrament of Healing through which we receive God's forgiveness through the ministry of the priest for the sins we commit after Baptism.

reparation [page 200]
The replacing or repairing of any harm we have caused by our words or actions

Resurrection [page 64]
The event of Jesus being raised from the dead to a new and glorified life.

Sabbath [page 192]
The seventh day of the week, the day Israelites dedicated and the Jewish people today dedicate to God as a holy day and day of rest.

sacraments [page 98]
The seven main liturgical signs of the Church, given to the Church by Jesus Christ, that make his saving work present and make us sharers in the life of God, the Holy Trinity.

Sacraments at the Service of Communion [pages 100, 146]
Holy Orders and Matrimony.

Sacraments of Healing [pages 100, 138–140]
Reconciliation, or Penance, and Anointing of the Sick.

Sacraments of Christian Initiation [pages 100, 111]
Baptism, Confirmation, and Eucharist.

Sacred Scripture [pages 22–25]
Two words that mean "holy writings"; the writings the Holy Spirit inspired the people of God to write and that have been collected by the Church in the Bible.

Sacred Tradition [page 78]
The passing on of the teachings of Christ by the Church through the power and guidance of the Holy Spirit.

sacrifice [page 122]
Freely giving up something of value out of love for God.

sanctifying [page 175]
A word that means "making holy."

sanctifying grace [page 175]
The gift of God's life and love that makes us holy and helps us live holy lives.

Sermon on the Mount [page 166]
The teachings of Jesus that are grouped together in chapters 5, 6, and 7 of the Gospel of Matthew.

sexuality [page 199]
The gift of being male or female—a boy or a man, or a girl or a woman.

sin [page 176]
Freely choosing to do what we know is against God's will or freely choosing not to do something we know God wants us to do.

soul [page 48]
The spiritual dimension of the human person that never dies, or is immortal.

steward [page 229]
One who is given the responsibility to care for what belongs to another person.

T-Z

temptation [page 158]
Everything that tries to move us away from living a holy life.

Ten Commandments [page 190]
The laws of the Covenant revealed to Moses and the Israelites on Mount Sinai.

venial sin [page 176]
A sin less serious than a mortal sin; a sin that does not have all the three things necessary for a sin to be mortal.

virtues [page 160]
Spiritual powers or habits or behaviors that help us do what is right and avoid what is wrong.

Word of God [page 16]
Title given to Jesus, the Son of God; the Bible, which is the inspired word of God.

worshiping assembly [page 124]
The community of the new People of God, the Church, joined with Christ gathered to give praise and thanks to God the Father through the power of the Holy Spirit.

Index

Credits

CPSIA information can be obtained
at www.ICGtesting.com
Printed in the USA
LVHW050301170720
660887LV00002B/8